T0307247

AIN'T GOT A BARREL OF MONEY

SHEFFIELD UNITED

AIN'T GOT A BARREL OF MONEY

SHEFFIELD UNITED

JASON HOLYHEAD

pitch

First published by Pitch Publishing, 2022

Pitch Publishing
A2 Yeoman Gate
Yeoman Way
Worthing
Sussex
BN13 3QZ
www.pitchpublishing.co.uk
info@pitchpublishing.co.uk

© 2022, Jason Holyhead

Every effort has been made to trace the copyright.
Any oversight will be rectified in future editions at the earliest opportunity by the publisher.

All rights reserved. No part of this book may be reproduced, sold or utilised in any form or transmitted in any form or by any means, electronic or mechanical, including photocopying, recording or by any information storage and retrieval system, without prior permission in writing from the Publisher.

A CIP catalogue record is available for this book from the British Library.

ISBN 978 1 80150 060 9

Typesetting and origination by Pitch Publishing

Printed and bound in Great Britain by TJ Books, Padstow

Contents

Foreword by Alan Biggs

AS SOMEONE with the incredible luck to have spent a working lifetime meeting stars of sport, the thrill never wears off. That sense of awe can be conquered to enable you to do your job, but it never leaves you completely.

And thankfully so, because it is part of that job to be enraptured by your subject. How can you convey it to those less fortunate if you lose that sense of wonder?

This is the story of a football supporter's discovery of that same precious feeling as he tracks down some of his heroes of Sheffield United.

While observing strict impartiality on the Sheffield scene myself, I'll never forget the door I knocked on very early in my career or the person who opened it. There had been rumours of the Blades' biggest star leaving for Leeds (as he subsequently did) and I set off to do that very old-fashioned thing of daring to go and see him.

Wouldn't happen now and feels like an invasion of privacy, to be honest. I'm no advocate of doorstepping, let me add! But the man who appeared in a smart, open-necked pink shirt at his home in Dronfield took it all in his stride. He was more polite than he needed to be in the circumstances. Didn't tell me much, mind you. But that didn't matter. I had met Tony Currie!

Some people say never meet your heroes for fear of being disappointed. I have seldom found that to be true and TC was a personal hero for the way he played, never mind that I supported ... Chesterfield. Amazingly, I'd now regard him as a friend after numerous interviews.

The wonderful Bramall Lane era of Currie and Woody (Alan Woodward) is at the centre of this narrative, which rightly pays particular homage to the humble man who created it, John Harris, one of the three greatest Blades bosses of my memory, along with Dave Bassett and Chris Wilder.

I'll never forget, either, the fateful day that all too swiftly followed when I made the mistake of presenting my Sportacular programme from Rotherham United's 1981 promotion party at Millmoor, little imagining that there would be a much more newsworthy relegation wake at S2.

United's incredible rise and fall across an eventful decade, from the summit of the First Division to the Fourth, is a tale that demands re-telling, warts and all. In this book, the story is given an added, special dimension by Jason Holyhead – the chance for Sheffield United fans to see worshipped figures through the eyes of one of their own.

I imagine Jason set off on his mission somewhat starry-eyed. I hope that is still the case. Thankfully we always have clearer recall of a bright sunny day than a 'walk in the rain'.

You can be sure Jason has put a barrel-load of love into this project – and I am sure that it will truly fill up your senses!

INTRODUCTION

Ain't Got a Barrel of Money. Sheffield United

THE METEORIC rise of Sheffield United to the Premier League was, for many, a surprise. When Chris Wilder took over the club that he had supported from the terraces as a boy, at a ground where he had been a ball boy as a kid and a player as a younger man – the Blades were languishing in League One.

Years of mediocrity had seen the club he loved sitting in the lower divisions for far too long. United had been languishing in the third tier for five seasons, since slipping out of the Championship in 2011. United won just 43 points in that season.

Wilder took charge on 12 May 2016 after the club parted company with Nigel Adkins. United had finished 11th in League One under Adkins the previous season, three points behind Gillingham and Rochdale: a position that was simply not acceptable for the fans or the club.

In Wilder's first season at the Lane, his team won promotion to the Championship, gaining 100 points and the league title en route. The following season – back in the Championship – was no failure either. United were at the top end of the table for much of the season until a serious injury to midfielder Paul Coutts coincided with a drop in form and subsequent drop down the table, eventually finishing a respectable tenth, five places above local rivals Wednesday.

The following season, Wilder built on the previous campaign's success and won promotion, United's second in three years, finishing second behind Norwich City and five points above third-placed Leeds, who eventually missed out on promotion in the play-offs.

Considerable investment in the team over the summer, with the acquisition of several players that repeatedly broke the club's transfer records, saw the Blades as high as fifth in the Premier League in November 2019, just a place behind reigning champions Manchester City.

The January 2020 transfer window saw further investment in the squad, breaking the club's transfer record again, this time to bring in Norwegian, Sander Berge.

Come mid-February's winter break, United were astonishingly still fifth, just two points behind fourth-placed Chelsea, with the prospect of European football for the first time in the club's history still a possibility.

When the season was paused due to the Covid-19 outbreak, the Blades sat seventh in the Premier League – level on points with sixth-placed Wolves, and two points behind Manchester United in fifth, with a game in hand on both.

A poor restart and what, at best, might be called a technology glitch, against Aston Villa – which resulted in one point, rather than three – saw United finish the season in ninth place, just two points behind Arsenal. What followed in the second season back in the top flight was nothing short of disastrous. With no fans in the ground in 2020/21 and a seemingly ever-growing injury list, United spent the season at the foot of the league table. The final blow was Wilder's departure.

The last five years under Chris Wilder were undoubtedly – for a generation of fans – the best period in United's recent history. Of course, fans of different generations will have their own opinions of when the golden era was for Sheffield United Football Club.

Each fan will have his or her own favourite player: perhaps Jimmy Hagan, Doc Pace, Len Badger, Tony Currie, Alan Woodward or Mick Speight; or for slightly younger fans, the best players might be Keith Edwards, Colin Morris, Glyn Hodges or Brian Deane, who scored the first ever goal of the Premier League era.

Now, there will be a brand-new generation of fans whose favourite players will be Chris Basham, Billy Sharp or John Fleck.

Those same fans will also of course have their own opinions on the worst period of the club's history, but there is little doubt that the darkest day in the long and occasionally illustrious history of Sheffield United Football Club, was the day they were relegated to the old Fourth Division.

Under Wilder, and his assistant Alan Knill, those days seemed a distant memory, as United approached the top flight fearlessly, but some fans will remember that we have been here before.

When football restarted after the enforced Covid break, it was a very different Sheffield United that limped to the end of the 2019/20 season. The second season, behind closed doors, was a disaster. Bottom of the league from the outset, United never recovered. Eventually, the unthinkable happened and Chris Wilder left the club, much to the dismay of most fans.

The inevitable relegation followed soon afterwards. There was a point during the season that United looked likely to break all the unwanted records available: lowest goals tally, lowest number of points – the list went on and on. Somehow, under interim manager Paul Heckingbottom, United managed to avoid most of the records, but the relegation signalled the end of an era.

Before this current crop of heroes were born, Sheffield United had a colourful history, filled with promise, glory, success and failure.

There have been highs and there have been lows. There have been great nights of celebration and tears of absolute frustration and utter disappointment. There has been controversy and there has been joy.

In this book we go back to a different era; decades ago, before the Premier League, before every game was televised, before massive money was paid to our heroes, before we had 24-hour access to them via social media; before bloody VAR …

Chapter 1

BETWEEN 1955 and 1959, Joe Mercer was the manager of Sheffield United Football Club, having taken over when Reg Freeman died during the close season. Mercer had enjoyed a distinguished career as a player, starting at Everton, in a team that included the wonderful Dixie Dean, before moving to Arsenal – where he won an FA Cup winner's medal.

He was so well thought of at Highbury, that there was a media campaign to make him the Gunners' manager but that did not materialise. He also represented his country on five occasions as a player.

Mercer's first shot at management was less spectacular – relegated in his first season in charge of the Blades. Mercer had little or no experience in the Second Division, and even less experience of man-management. But, after the initial disappointment, he started to put together a decent youth set-up at United and made good use of some of the many contacts he had made during his playing days.

Before his efforts could come to fruition, Mercer decided he needed to be at a bigger club, and in December 1958 he resigned, to manage Aston Villa. He took Villa down in his first season as their manager as well.

Following relegation, Mercer built a decent young team, nicknamed 'Mercer's Minors' in the press. His talented young Aston Villa side won promotion to the First Division as champions in 1959/60 by playing bold, exciting football.

In the 1960/61 season his side lifted the League Cup. He was extremely busy, not only in team affairs but also being involved in the development of the ground. The workload took its toll and in 1964 Mercer suffered a stroke. Somewhat insensitively, after his recovery Aston Villa terminated his contract.

A year later, initially against doctors' orders, he moved to Manchester City. His doctors later admitted to his wife Norah, 'He may as well die doing something he loves, as sit at home and die of a broken heart.'

Fearing people doubted him due to his health problems, Mercer appointed a young and flamboyant Malcolm Allison as his assistant. Norah played a big part too. She often mothered the players, making sure they had eaten properly and were being looked after by the club.

Mercer and Allison enjoyed much success at City, and they arguably became the most entertaining team of that era. Mercer had met Allison, a larger-than-life extrovert, at an FA coaching session. He said later, 'The chance [to work with Allison] was irresistible. I knew that people had written me off. There were doubts over my health, but I had no lack of confidence in my ability. Allison was magnificent. I knew we had a chance at Manchester City. Although they were Second Division, they were a club with tradition and a ready-made public.'

City won promotion to the First Division in 1966 and in '68 they won the league. It was a remarkably short journey from a mid-table Second Division side to league champions, in just three years.

As Allison's reputation grew, so too did his ambition, and he wanted to be in control of Manchester City. A boardroom split over ownership and who should be the manager gave fuel to this. Peter Swales wanted to run the club and Allison backed him, apparently under the promise of getting the manager's job.

Mercer sided with the existing board, and when Swales won, the end was in sight for Mercer. He wanted to carry on at the club he had achieved so much with so quickly, and the fans undoubtedly felt the same way, so the club reached a compromise – Allison would take on the manager's role and Mercer would assume the role of general manager.

Mercer, however, on finding he had lost his parking space and office at the ground, decided enough was enough. In June 1971 he resigned from the club, ending the most celebrated period in Manchester City's history.

Mercer left Maine Road as the most successful City manager of all time, and despite the treatment he had received from the board, the fans recognised his contribution and shortly after his departure they invited him to attend their annual ceremony, where they presented him with a silver tea service.

His wife Norah was so well appreciated that years later, when she died, several members of the Manchester City team and other well-known players attended her funeral.

After his resignation at City, Mercer moved to Coventry City. During his time as Coventry boss, he spent seven games as caretaker-manager of the England team, in 1974, after Sir

Alf Ramsey left following England's failure to qualify for the 1974 World Cup.

He approached the England job with much the same style as he had his club football, doing it the Joe Mercer way by picking flair players such as Frank Worthington and Stan Bowles. His record as England supremo was so good that there was talk of him getting the job permanently, but the FA opted for former Leeds United manager Don Revie instead.

Mercer received an OBE for services to football in 1976. At the old Maine Road ground of Manchester City there was a suite named after him and following their move to the Etihad, a street was named in his honour – Joe Mercer Way.

Joe Mercer OBE passed away on his 76th birthday after suffering from Alzheimer's.

At Bramall Lane, on Mercer's exit, coach Archie Clarke had been put in temporary charge of the Blades, and when John Harris arrived in the spring of 1959, he inherited a good foundation of a team that was in need of strengthening, but he also inherited a formidable defence.

Cec Coldwell, Brian Richardson, the Shaws – Graham and Joe – and Gerry Summers, in front of Alan Hodgkinson in goal, formed a solid base for Harris to build on.

United had made a poor start to the season under Mercer but had climbed to fifth by the time he quit. Archie Clarke had overseen four consecutive victories in January and into the start of February, adding two more wins following a 2-2 draw away at Arsenal in the fifth round of the FA Cup. United beat them 3-0 in the replay and a 1-0 win over Wednesday continued the run.

Norwich City put an end to United's cup run in early March – again in a replay, after a 1-1 draw in the first game. The Canaries ran out 2-3 winners at the second attempt.

Two further defeats in a row followed the exit from the cup, before United rallied and went on a run which saw them lose just once in 13 games, before Harris was appointed. The end of the season saw a rather good third-place finish, but Wednesday were champions, nine points ahead of the Blades.

The 1959/60 campaign was to be John Harris's first full season in charge. He was hugely different to his predecessor. Glasgow-born Harris always dressed in a suit and tie and did not drink, smoke or swear, and was often referred to as Gentleman John.

He followed his father's footsteps into football. His dad was a Newcastle United centre-forward, who also managed Swindon Town and Swansea City. John Harris started playing at centre-back for Swindon Town before moving to Swansea, then to Spurs, Wolves and Southampton, before a transfer to Chelsea, where he captained the Blues to win the First Division championship in 1955. He left Chelsea to take up a player-manager role at Chester in 1956.

On his appointment at Bramall Lane, Harris retained the services of coach and chief scout, Archie Clarke, who had brought some great young talent to the club, as well as doing an admirable job of holding the reins since Mercer's departure.

The season started positively. Friendlies against Dutch clubs SC Enschede and PSV Eindhoven both ended in wins, and an opening-day league win at home to Derby County preceded a 6-0 thrashing of Hull City. Doc Pace scored twice, Willie Hamilton added another two, and Harris's Blades were off and running.

Cec Coldwell missed the Hull game through injury and would not play in the next seven games, Cliff Mason deputising. Coldwell returned for the home game against Bristol City on 19 September. United won 5-2 and Pace netted his fourth league goal of the season.

An away trip to Scunthorpe United the following week saw Pace score his fifth in a 1-1 draw. Bernard Shaw was injured in that game and Mason came back in for the next game, at home to South Yorkshire neighbours, Rotherham United (Mason had been signed to cover for Shaw while he was serving in the army). The Blades lost 2-3 but Pace was on target again.

A midweek friendly against Swiss side Lucerne saw Pace score two of United's five goals, before he scored yet again in a 1-1 draw with his previous club, Aston Villa.

Derek Pace came from a footballing family. His father, Charles, had managed Essington Villa in the 1930s, and his mother was part of a ladies' team that played games for charity.

Derek signed for Aston Villa in 1949 but was called up to carry out his national service almost straight away. He served in the medical corps, which is where the nickname 'Doc' came from. Doc, although not the biggest centre-forward, was tough and had great awareness in the penalty area and could time his runs wonderfully. He was a two-footed player and could head the ball equally as efficiently.

When Pace returned to Villa after his National Service, they had a wealth of strikers at the club and he found games hard to come by, but despite only playing in half a dozen games, he scored six goals, including one on his debut.

Mercer had fancied Pace for a while, but Villa had been reluctant to let him go. However, he finally signed for United on the morning of Boxing Day 1957.

He made his Blades debut that very afternoon and repeated what he had done at Villa, scoring in his first game, a 4-2 win over Blackburn Rovers. United had another game two days later against Lincoln City, in which Pace scored again, making him an instant favourite with the Bramall Lane faithful.

Although he joined United halfway through the season, he netted 15 times in 19 games. In his first full season he scored an impressive 26 in the league, as well as three FA Cup goals and his tally at the end of 1958/59 was 34.

Now aged 27, Pace was in the form of his life, and two days after scoring against his former club again, he scored two against Sheffield Wednesday in a 3-1 win in the County Cup.

That week, Harold MacMillan secured a third term in office for his party, as the Tories won a General Election with a massive majority. Although he had been a member of Parliament since 1931, it was MacMillan's first election as leader and his Conservatives won 365 seats to Labour's 258.

In victory MacMillan declared, 'This election has shown that the class war is obsolete.' Defeated Labour leader Hugh Gaitskell commented, 'We have attacked and on this occasion were repulsed. We shall attack again, and again and again until we win.'

Back-to-back defeats followed the win over rivals Wednesday, but United got back to winning ways by beating Huddersfield Town 0-1 and Ipswich Town by the same margin – Billy Russell getting both goals.

Form was indifferent in November and United won two, lost one and drew one. December had a similar theme, with

United losing to Stoke City and Cardiff City. However, the new year would see an upturn in form, and United beat Plymouth Argyle 4-0 on 2 January 1960, before losing just once in the next ten games.

Three wins in their last three league fixtures of the season saw a decent fourth-place finish behind Aston Villa, Cardiff City and Liverpool. Pace finished the season as United's top scorer on 33 goals.

Chapter 2

TWO PRE-SEASON friendlies in Holland again saw back-to-back wins for United, scoring five in each game. Pace grabbed a goal in each. The new, 1960/61 season got under way at Norwich City, where Hamilton scored the equaliser in the second half of a 1-1 draw.

United's first home game of the season was a Tuesday night encounter with Plymouth Argyle. United ran out 3-0 victors, Pace getting his first of the season and Russell and Bill Hodgson opened their accounts. Pace was on target again the following Saturday at home to Charlton Athletic in a 1-0 win.

Defeat to Plymouth Argyle the following week, and then away at Stoke City would be United's only losses in a 13-game run, in which the Blades won ten. A 0-2 loss to Bury in the League Cup interrupted the run, but United won five out of the next six. However, a dismal run from late November into December left John Harris worried after his team failed to win in half a dozen attempts.

On 10 November 1960, book shops all over Britain sold out of copies of *Lady Chatterley's Lover.* DH Lawrence's raunchy novel sold 200,000 copies on the first day it went on sale, following Penguin winning the right to publish the work. Those lucky enough to get their hands on a copy had to pay 3s 6d. W&G Foyle, London's biggest bookshop at the time, sold 300 copies in the first 15 minutes. Selfridges sold 250 copies in a minute. Within a year, *Lady Chatterley's Lover* had sold two million copies, even out-selling the Bible.

That opening-day goal against Norwich City turned out to be Hamilton's only goal of the season. He missed some games through injury and his form was poor, so Harris brought in Keith Kettleborough from Rotherham United for £15,000. After shuffling his formation and initially trying Billy Russell out wide, he moved him back to inside-forward. Kettleborough didn't make much of an impression though and was also soon injured and only featured in eight games.

On New Year's Eve, United ended the terrible run by beating Charlton Athletic 3-2. Harris's Blades were then unbeaten in January, winning two league matches sandwiched between an FA Cup third-round tie against Everton and a fourth-round win over Lincoln City, Russell scoring in both.

On 20 January 1961, John Fitzgerald Kennedy became the 35th President of the United States of America. The 34-year-old closed his acceptance address with, 'Ask not what your country can do for you, ask what you can do for your country.'

Defeat away at Swansea City was a blip, but Russell was on the scoresheet again in a 2-1 win over Luton Town, and a 2-1

FA Cup fifth-round victory against Blackburn Rovers. A 5-0 thrashing of Lincoln City saw Russell add his fifth goal in five games and Doc Pace scored one, while Kettleborough chipped in with his first two goals since signing.

A Billy Russell hat-trick against Newcastle United continued United's FA Cup run, putting them through to the semi-finals, where they would meet First Division Leicester City. That, however, proved a step too far, and City beat United during a largely winless March for the Blades, except for a 2-1 victory over Yorkshire rivals Leeds United.

After a 1-1 draw with Liverpool, United went on to win the next four, beating Portsmouth, Rotherham United, Southampton and Derby County. The 3-1 defeat to Bristol Rovers would be the last of the season, as United beat Middlesbrough 4-1 in the final game of the campaign. Pace scored two, taking his haul for the season – in which he played in every game – to 32. Len Allchurch grabbed one while Russell netted his 25th of the season.

The season was a huge success. United were promoted to the First Division, finishing just a point behind champions Ipswich Town. Going up, getting to the semi-finals of the FA Cup and beating Leeds twice, is a good season by anyone's standards.

John Harris was so pleased with his side, that he decided not to strengthen in the summer and would go into the First Division with the same team that got them there.

Division Two table 1960/61

	Played	*W*	*D*	*L*	*Points*
1 Ipswich Town	42	26	7	9	59
2 Sheffield United	42	26	6	10	58

The annual pre-season trip to Holland would not have dulled Harris's belief, as United comfortably beat MVV Maastricht 3-1 before a 5-0 demolition of DWS Amsterdam. Doc Pace got two in the second game and one in the first; Billy Russell also scored in both games.

Sheffield United's first home game back in Division One was watched by 27,932 fans as United ran out 2-1 winners. Level at half-time, Hodgson sent the Blades fans home happy, grabbing the winner against Wolverhampton Wanderers.

A 1-1 draw with Cardiff City and defeat away at Nottingham Forest brought the Blades back down to earth. The fixture lists could throw up some anomalies in those days, and United faced Cardiff again for the second time in five days. Allchurch scored the winner in a 1-0 win, but United suffered their second loss of the season, away at Aston Villa, then drew 1-1 with Spurs before an absolute trouncing at Chelsea. Pace scored in the first half but an awful second half saw Chelsea score five goals – not the ideal preparation for their next game, a local derby against Wednesday.

United had won just two of their opening eight games back in the top division. They had scored six goals and conceded 13. Wednesday were in good form and had lost just once, away at Bolton Wanderers. They had scored 19 goals in their opening eight games and let in just eight. Close to 40,000 were at Bramall Lane to see Derek Pace's winner in the Steel City derby. Wednesday would remain winless for the rest of September, while United won two of their next three, with Pace getting five goals.

Pace scored again in a 2-2 draw with Newcastle United and Allchurch got one as United went down 1-4 at Leicester City.

A 2-0 win at Newcastle, this time in the League Cup second round, preceded an excellent 2-1 home victory against Ipswich Town, who would go on to win the title.

The second half of October was less productive and after winning a friendly 3-0 against West Germany's Eintracht Frankfurt, United lost at Goodison Park, were held 2-2 by Fulham, and lost 2-0 at Bolton Wanderers, on the day before Bonfire Night. In contrast, the remainder of November and December were very good. Seven wins in their next nine games would lift spirits and see United start to climb the table. Ronnie Simpson, netting five times during that run, eased the pressure on Pace, although United still depended heavily on their talisman's goals.

In January, a third-round FA Cup tie with Bury would take three meetings before United eventually beat them 2-0 in the second replay, with Pace getting both goals. Further victories against Chelsea and a fourth-round FA Cup match against Peterborough United, saw Pace get another two, leading up to the away game at Wednesday.

This time United were in a much better state and two more goals from the irrepressible Pace in front of 50,000 at Hillsborough on 3 February 1962 meant Blades fans could enjoy a special Sheffield double.

It would be March before United lost, in a humbling 4-0 defeat to the excellent Ipswich Town. Defeat in the quarter-finals of the FA Cup at home to Burnley, and a 5-2 loss to Fulham would follow, and a fifth-round exit from the League Cup, losing 2-0 to Blackpool. A 1-1 draw at Manchester City ended a miserable March.

Victory over Blackpool away and draws against West Bromwich Albion and Tottenham, before losing 3-0 away at Birmingham City, saw little improvement in April, before back-to-back wins against Burnley and Manchester United.

A disappointing 2-0 defeat to Arsenal in the closing game of the season left United fifth in Division One, just four points behind Everton. Nonetheless, it was an impressive first season back in the big league. By reaching the quarter-finals in both cups and doing the double over the Owls, who finished a place behind the Blades, the good times had arrived.

Pace finished the season with a remarkable 41 goals in all competitions.

Ipswich Town, who had pipped United to the Division Two title the previous year, claimed the Division One title, qualifying for the European Cup. Alf Ramsey was the Ipswich manager at the time but left in 1963 to manage the England side. When he took over the role at Ipswich in August 1955, they had been in the old Division Three (South). They won that league in 1956/57 to begin their climb to the top. In the European Cup, Ipswich beat Floriana 14-1 on aggregate, but were later knocked out by AC Milan.

Ramsey's successes at Ipswich were a remarkable achievement and were possibly only ever bettered by him leading his country to World Cup glory in 1966.

Division One table 1961/62

	Played	*W*	*D*	*L*	*Points*
1 Ipswich Town	42	24	8	10	56
2 Burnley	42	21	11	10	53
3 Tottenham	42	21	10	11	52
4 Everton	42	20	11	11	51
5 Sheffield Utd	42	19	9	14	47

Chapter 3

BUOYED BY his team's relative success in their first season in the top division, Harris was confident that his experienced defence and guaranteed goals from Pace would be sufficient, and again he didn't sign any players during the 1962 pre-season. He did, however, introduce some of the successful youth system that the club had been developing.

An opening-day defeat at Nottingham Forest saw Pace add to the three goals he had scored in pre-season friendlies in Holland. Back-to-back wins against Fulham and reigning champions Ipswich Town ensured a decent start, Pace scoring again in the latter. United then drew 2-2 away at Fulham before going down 2-0 at Anfield.

Back at Bramall Lane, Pace scored again in a 1-1 draw with Blackburn Rovers and in a 2-1 defeat, at home to Wolves. Barry Hartle scored twice in a 2-1 win at Aston Villa and Pace got his name in the papers again, scoring his fifth of the season, away at Blackburn's Ewood Park.

At the end of September, riots broke out in Mississippi, resulting in two deaths and at least 75 people injured.

> The protestors were angry that James Meredith, a black American man, had been admitted to the university in the town of Oxford. Hundreds of extra troops were called in and President Kennedy called for a peaceful settlement to the dispute. Mr Meredith is said to have remained calm and dignified throughout the disturbance. He said at the time, 'This is more for America, than for me.' He completed his two years at the campus, despite being shunned and isolated, and graduated with a degree in political science. He would later earn a law degree and was pivotal in the civil rights movement.

The Blades made it four wins in a row, beating Spurs 3-1 and Brentford 4-1 in the League Cup. Graham Shaw scored a penalty away at West Ham United to secure a 1-1 draw, before the trip to Hillsborough on 6 October. Shaw again converted from the spot and Doc Pace got another goal against the Owls. The game finished 2-2.

A trip to Burnley on 13 October ended in a heavy 5-1 defeat. United showed some resilience, and in the next game ran out 4-1 winners at home to Bolton Wanderers, Pace again on the scoresheet. A League Cup third-round match at Bury, which United lost 3-1, saw a young Len Badger step in to replace veteran Cec Coldwell.

Further defeats to Leicester City away, Birmingham City at home and Arsenal away, would see United score just one league goal in three games. Respite came in the shape of a 1-0 win at home to West Bromwich Albion on 17 November.

The winter was a harsh one, the worst since the 1940s, and many games were postponed. The FA Cup third-round game wouldn't take place until March. In December, Manchester

United came to Bramall Lane and earned a point, Simpson scoring from the spot for the Blades. Another draw followed at Leyton Orient, this time Shaw from the spot and Pace adding the other.

The following week, Pace grabbed a brace against Nottingham Forest and a Friday night match on 21 December saw the Blades lose 1-0 at Ipswich Town. It was almost a month before United resumed playing, when they travelled to Wolves on 19 January, to draw 0-0 – but that was the only game they played throughout January.

United went into the new year mid-table and in mid-February, they were beaten 2-0 away at West Ham United. Three wins on the bounce followed, with United seeing off Stoke City and Burnley without conceding and then beat Bolton Wanderers in that long-awaited FA Cup third-round game, 3-1. The fourth-round tie was played less than a week later and United progressed again, beating Port Vale 2-1. Three days later, United played their fourth game in two weeks and lost 0-1 to Southampton – ending their FA Cup run for another year.

With the fixtures coming thick and fast in March, United travelled to Birmingham City to win 1-0, and drew 0-0 at home to Leicester City, before beating Everton 2-1. Manchester City came to Bramall Lane on Wednesday, 3 April, and found Derek Pace in unstoppable form. The Sheffield United goal machine netted a hat-trick, his 15th, 16th and 17th goals of the season, in a 3-1 win.

The following Saturday, United travelled to the Hawthorns, where they beat West Bromwich Albion 2-1. A 3-3 draw at home to Arsenal saw Allchurch convert two penalties to complete his hat-trick.

The draw with the Gunners was the first of four games without a win for the Blades. Wagstaff scored a consolation goal in a 3-1 defeat at Blackpool, before drawing to the same team the next day, and again, away at Manchester United, in a game in which young Mick Jones made his debut, aged 17.

Four days later, United beat the other Manchester team – City – 3-1, Pace scoring his fourth goal in a month against them. Jones scored twice, his first goals for the club, on the day of his 18th birthday.

Jones was born in Shireoaks, Nottinghamshire and was spotted playing for Dinnington Miners Welfare. He was snapped up by the Blades and had been playing in the Central League, along with other promising youngsters, including Len Badger.

Badger made his league debut, in place of Coldwell, as he had in the League Cup earlier in the season, and Bernard Shaw – younger brother of Graham – played his first game against Leyton Orient, Jones and Hartle scoring for United without reply. After keeping a clean sheet against Orient, Badger and Shaw might have felt hard done by when Coldwell and Shaw Sr came back into the team the following week against Aston Villa. This time Pace and Wagstaff scored in the 2-1 win.

United failed to win any of their final three games of the season, including a 3-1 defeat to Wednesday on the final day of the campaign, and finished tenth in the table. That position was not as high as the previous season, but still a decent performance for a team in only their second season back in the top flight.

Pace finished as United's top scorer again with 25 and the development and introduction of Badger, Shaw, Wagstaff and Jones were more reasons to be cheerful.

Everton won the league, six points clear of runners-up Spurs. Wednesday finished a respectable sixth, four points above United.

The 1963/64 season started again with little activity in the transfer market; Harris was confident that his squad was good enough, particularly with the evolving talents in the youth ranks.

Mick Jones, who had made his debut the previous season, had managed to hold on to the number ten jersey for the remainder of the season, after scoring four times. He started the new season up front alongside Derek Pace.

The perennial trip to Holland saw Pace get off the mark, and Allchurch scored in both games against DDS and ADD.

In the season opener, away at Blackpool, Pace scored his first league goal of the campaign, Simpson scoring the other in a 2-2 draw. A defeat at home to Blackburn Rovers and draws against Chelsea at home and then away at Blackburn got August off to a slow start.

> At the end of August, Martin Luther King told a crowd of over 250,000 people about his dream for freedom. He promised the huge gathering in Washington that the fight for equality would continue until 'justice rolls down like waters and righteousness, like a mighty stream'.

The draw against Chelsea would see Graham Shaw suffer an injury that would keep him out for five months, effectively ending the famous defensive line of the late 1950s.

Tony Wagstaff returned to the side after being consistently picked in the latter stages of the previous season. Wagstaff, a midfielder, born in nearby Wombwell, had joined United as an apprentice in 1960, but didn't break into the first team regularly until 1962/63. He was considered by some to lack the yard of pace needed to succeed, but his skill was plentiful, and he chipped in with a few goals.

A visit to the capital against West Ham United saw the Blades win for the first time in the new season, 3-2, with a goal from Wagstaff and two from Allchurch.

Allchurch was on target again the following week against Stoke City at home, United putting four past them. Pace scored two of the four. The next home game was against Wednesday and an unchanged line-up drew 1-1, with Simpson getting the goal for United. Wagstaff and Kettleborough scored a goal each away at Stoke City, before Wagstaff scored again against Liverpool back at Bramall Lane, Pace getting a double, taking his tally to six already.

A 2-1 defeat to Bolton Wanderers saw United make an early exit from the League Cup, in the second round, with Wagstaff again finding the net. Badger made his first start of the season. Parks deputised for Pace.

On 28 September, United travelled to Villa Park. Pace was recalled to the team and inevitably scored the winner against his former employers. Early October saw a thrilling encounter at Bramall Lane, when Wagstaff, Simpson and John Docherty scored. The game finished Sheffield United 3 Tottenham Hotspur 3.

Four days later, United beat Ipswich Town 3-1, Docherty netting twice, and Simpson also got on the scoresheet. Tony Wagstaff scored United's only goal away at Everton, as the Toffees put four past Hodgkinson.

The following week, Pace smashed in a hat-trick as the Blades beat Birmingham City 3-0 at Bramall Lane. A further win – away at Burnley – rounded off October, when Simpson scored both United's goals without reply. United won just once in November, 1-0 away at Filbert Street. Four defeats in a row followed.

On 22 November 1963, John F Kennedy, President of the United States of America, was shot dead. Lee Harvey Oswald was charged with his murder, but never reached court, as he too was shot dead two days later by nightclub owner, Jack Ruby. Conspiracy theorists still to this day, enjoy a variety of wild versions of the events. Ruby was sentenced to death for the killing of Oswald, but he also died before trial, after suffering an embolism.

On 14 December, United managed to stop the losing sequence by beating Blackpool 1-0 with an Allchurch penalty. That would be United's only victory in December though, meaning they had won just two of their last ten games.

In February, Cassius Clay won the heavyweight world title. The 22-year-old stopped Sonny Liston at the end of the sixth round, when Liston failed to get up off his stool.

An FA Cup third-round trip to Lincoln City was a welcome distraction for United and they won comfortably, 4-0, with Wagstaff on target, Hartle adding one and Mick Jones scoring twice. On 11 January, United beat West Ham United 2-1, Pace and Wagstaff with the goals.

It would be March before United tasted victory again.

The 3-0 defeat at Hillsborough on 18 January started that terrible run, and also marked the end of Gerry Summers's first-team career with the Blades. Summers had been signed by Joe Mercer from West Bromwich Albion in 1957. He played in over 260 games for United, before moving to Hull City. He later joined Walsall at the end of his career. When his playing career finished, he managed Oxford United until 1975 and then Gillingham. He also coached at Derby County and Leicester City.

Ken Mallender replaced Summers for the remainder of the season, while Graham Shaw – who had returned to the side in January – played as number nine against Burnley at the beginning of March, when United finally ended their winless streak with a 2-0 victory.

Shaw kept the number nine shirt for the next game, a 1-0 defeat at home to Leicester City. He then returned to his usual number three shirt, away at Arsenal. Allchurch grabbed two goals and Joe Shaw claimed one. Pace returned to the team against Arsenal and returned to the scoresheet two days later in a 1-1 draw with Wolves. Three wins and three losses in the remaining six fixtures left the Blades with a 12th-place finish.

Pace had missed too many games through injury but had still managed to finish as United's top scorer, for the sixth consecutive season, with 16 goals. Despite the much-anticipated emergence of the young talents Wagstaff, Jones and Badger, the team had not made progress, but rather the opposite, after a tenth-place finish the previous season, and fifth the year before that.

The reluctance of Harris to delve into the transfer market was, in part, due to the club's precarious financial situation. Harris declared that he would 'sooner persevere and try and bring in our boys'. It was said that Sheffield United needed an average attendance of 25,000 to meet the wage bill, but in the

1963/64 season the average had been little over 21,600 (this would decrease further over the next two seasons, although gate averages had increased since Harris's first season in charge and subsequent promotion).

The 1964/65 season began brightly, with the pre-season trip to Holland starting with a 3-1 win against DDS, but the second game, against Sparta, ended in a 4-0 defeat.

The Blades then lost their opening two league games against Tottenham and Stoke City without scoring. Allchurch was injured and would be replaced by John Docherty.

United tasted victory for the first time that season at home to Burnley on 29 August. Barry Hartle and Mick Jones got the goals. Stoke City were United's next opponents, but Derek Pace was ill, and Mick Jones took up the number nine shirt. He scored the only goal of the game and would retain the shirt for most of the season. The number ten shirt vacated by Jones was given to Alan Birchenall.

Birchenall had scored more than 60 goals for the juniors, and after just half a dozen games in the reserves, was thrust into the first team. In only his second game in a United shirt, against Wednesday at Hillsborough, he scored both goals in a 2-0 win, United's third victory on the bounce.

Two more wins followed two draws, seeing United unbeaten in seven fixtures, with Birchenall and Jones scoring seven goals between them. The Blades lost just one league game in a busy September – away at West Ham United. Birchenall would net eight times in his first nine appearances. He and Jones looked to be forging a formidable partnership and Pace would not regain his spot.

Derek Pace had been United's top scorer six seasons in a row. In 302 league and cup games, Doc scored 175 goals for the Blades. On leaving United, Pace signed for Notts County. He scored a further 15 goals for them in 29 games, before joining Walsall. He only managed a handful of games for Walsall but did score – with a flying header against Grimsby Town. By the time he hung up his boots, he had scored 233 goals in 444 games. He then walked away from football and went into sales in the Midlands.

Derek Pace passed away in October 1989.

A Wednesday night visit to Liverpool in October ended in a 3-1 defeat, but the game was memorable for one reason. John Docherty lost the number seven shirt to a young Alan Woodward. Woodward was another of the up-and-coming talents at the club. He had a fantastic ability to pass and shoot with power and accuracy. Chapeltown-born Woodward had made his first appearance for United in the County Cup against Rotherham United and played again in the final of that cup, against Barnsley.

The defeat at Anfield was the first of three consecutive losses before the Jones/Birchenall combination scored two apiece against Arsenal in a 4-0 win. The *Sunday Mirror* reported the following day that there was not a poor performer in the Sheffield United line-up, their youngest for years.

Tony Wagstaff's younger brother Barry broke into the team, to be the second debutant against Liverpool. While Barry Wagstaff's arrival was cut short by appendicitis, Woodward would become an instant favourite with the crowd. He kept his place in the side for the majority of the season.

The campaign was blighted by injury and illness, paving the way for more youngsters to come through, but the variations were not good for consistency and as the weeks went by, results suffered. Being second in the table in September became mid-table soon after.

United won just once in December, beating Aston Villa 4-2. A 3-3 draw at home to Spurs preceded a 1-3 defeat at Burnley. On Boxing Day, United hosted Manchester United. Sheffield United lost 0-1.

The first game of 1965 was at home to Sheffield Wednesday, on 2 January. Birchenall and defender Reg Matthewson scored for United, but Wednesday won 2-3. United remained winless throughout January but won consecutive games at the beginning of February, against West Ham United and West Bromwich Albion. They drew the other two games in February, against Blackpool and then Blackburn Rovers respectively, and extended the unbeaten run to seven games at the start of March. A Barry Hartle equaliser earned the Blades a point at Highbury, before Hartle, Woodward and Birchenall all scored at home to Liverpool.

The victory at home to Liverpool would be followed by a disastrous run of nine games without a win. Scoring just twice, United suffered six consecutive defeats, a draw at Nottingham Forest and further defeats in the last two league fixtures resulting in a poor 19th-position finish.

Early exits from both cups compounded the poor season, but the development of Badger, Woodward, Jones and Birchenall forming the basis of a very young but talented Sheffield United side, was at least encouraging.

At the end of a disappointing season, United used the money they had received for Len Allchurch – who they sold in March to fourth tier Stockport County – and made a rare exception to their transfer policy, when they bought Gil Reece from Newport County. Reece, a clever, fast, and strong outside-left, had represented Wales at schoolboy level, and an excellent 1964/65 season with Newport County caught Harris's attention. United paid £10,000 for him.

Instead of the regular trip to Holland for pre-season friendlies, United stayed on home soil before the 1965/66 season. Reece scored twice on his debut against Doncaster Rovers, and again in the 1-1 draw with Derby County. A 4-2 win away at Huddersfield Town completed pre-season.

Graham Shaw was replaced by Ken Mallender for the season opener, which United won 1-0 at home to Aston Villa in front of 15,575 supporters. United won by the same margin at Anfield four days later, Jones scoring his first of the season.

The Blades were on the wrong end of a 4-1 scoreline at Sunderland's Roker Park, in front of 42,147 fans. The home crowd was again just over 15,700 in September, when United soundly beat West Ham 5-3; Birchenall scored his second of the season, Docherty and Kettleborough grabbed one each and Mick Jones scored two.

Badger scored one in a 2-0 win over Fulham and Birchenall scored the winner again against Wednesday in front of Bramall Lane's biggest crowd of the season, 35,655.

United were top of the league at the start of October, but inconsistency put paid to that. Three defeats in a row meant they dropped off top spot. On 6 November Reece scored one and Jones added another in the second half, but unfortunately Arsenal led 4-1 at half-time and added two more after the break. The following week, at home to Everton, Mick Jones scored both goals in a 2-0 win for United.

At the end of November, Woodward scored a penalty and Jones and Wagstaff both scored in a 3-2 win against Newcastle

United. In December, the Blades failed to register a victory in the league, and it would be 15 January before they would win again. That win came at home to Burnley, Woodward and Reece scoring the goals. Woodward was on target again in the FA Cup third round against Fulham – two goals from Birchenall confirming the win.

Reece scored both goals in a 2-0 victory over Aston Villa to make it three wins in a row in January. It was a month that also saw Badger captain the side. A 3-0 defeat at Wolves ended United's FA Cup run, before they went down 4-0 at Upton Park.

Inconsistency continued in March, as United won two, lost two and drew 2-2 against the Owls. Birchenall, of course, scored both United's goals at Hillsborough. That form continued into April and the Blades lost two but won their last three league games, to finish a respectable ninth in Division One.

Birchenall's six goals in four games against bitter rivals Wednesday were appreciated by the fans, but his tally for the season was 13 in all competitions and United relied far too heavily on Mick Jones's goals, his total of 21 in the league was almost as many as the rest of the entire team scored. Reece scored seven of the 34 goals the others contributed.

1966 would, of course, be the first and so far only time England won the FIFA World Cup. The group stage of the tournament was not a high-scoring affair. England topped their group after scoring four goals and conceding none.

In the quarter-finals, England beat Argentina 1-0 after Antonio Rattin became the first player to be sent off in a senior international match at Wembley Stadium. Boca Juniors legend Rattin refused to leave the field and eventually had to be escorted off by police officers.

The semi-final was moved from Goodison Park to Wembley, and England beat Portugal – Bobby Charlton scoring both of England's goals. The great Eusebio ended England's clean sheet from the penalty spot. West Germany played their semi-final at Goodison and beat Russia 2-1.

On 30 July, England faced West Germany at Wembley Stadium. The massive crowd of 98,000 saw Helmut Haller put the Germans in front. Less than five minutes later Geoff Hurst levelled for England. Martin Peters put England in front with just ten minutes left on the clock, but Wolfgang Weber equalised in the last minute of normal time.

What happened in extra time is known to every football fan in the country. Hurst scored his second when his shot hit the underneath of the crossbar and bounced on the line. The debate about whether it crossed the line, and whether VAR would have allowed it rages on to this day. England's fourth, and Hurst's third was indisputable. Kenneth Wolstenholme's 'Some people are on the pitch' is one of the most famous pieces of football commentary ever.

While fans around the world watched Bobby Moore lift the most coveted trophy in sport, the people of Sheffield watched the Bramall Lane end being turned into a two-tier stand, costing in the region of £100,000.

Unsurprisingly, John Harris didn't strengthen his squad, despite selling Docherty, Kettleborough and Brian Richardson midway through the previous season. Richardson had signed for the Blades some 12 years earlier, aged 20. Now 32 and having played in 300-plus games in that magnificent defence, he was sold to Swindon Town.

Born and raised in Sheffield, Richardson passed away, aged 85, in 2020.

Goalkeeper Alan Hodgkinson was starting his tenth season as a regular for the Blades. He had joined in 1954 under Reg Freeman, but had begun to establish himself in the first team in the back half of the 1956/57 season.

Len Badger was made captain of Sheffield United for the 1966/67 season. He had made the right-back position his own, replacing the long-serving Cec Coldwell and now he had replaced Joe Shaw as captain.

Shaw had played in over 600 games for the Blades but hadn't featured since February 1966 (when Badger first took over as captain) and took up a coaching role with the team. He would later move on to be manager of York City and Chesterfield.

With a couple of exceptions, including the outstanding Gil Reece, Badger led a team that had been completely home grown by United and almost all of them came from Sheffield or the surrounding areas. They were undoubtedly a talented but fairly small group and with the odd exception, were inexperienced.

With no additions to the squad, United would need to hope for a relatively injury-free campaign. Substitutions had been introduced the previous season, but each team was only permitted to make one change, and this had to be due to injury. Tactical substitutions were not permitted.

United spent pre-season in England again, playing three away games. Facing Stockport County in the first game, United won 2-0, Reece and Birchenall scoring the goals. Reece was on target again in the second friendly, a 1-1 draw at Oldham Athletic.

The third friendly was against Brighton and Hove Albion. The game finished 1-1, the brilliant Alan Woodward on target for United. This was not a marvellous warm-up. None of the teams United faced were in the same division, and United had only won one of the games. Against Oldham Athletic, Harris made one change to his line-up, replacing Mexborough-born Frank Barlow with Sheffield-born David Munks, but Barlow had returned for the trip to Brighton.

Harris made one change to the starting XI for the first league game of the season, away at Burnley: Brian Shaw was replaced by Ken Mallender. United were thrashed 4-0 after being level at half-time.

Harris had confidence in his young team's ability and kept them unchanged in the second game, which was three days later at home to Newcastle United. Newcastle won 1-0. The following week, United travelled to Nottingham Forest – Shaw was recalled to the starting XI, but United lost 1-0. Another defeat away at Newcastle United ended in the same result as their previous meeting, 1-0 to Newcastle. United had lost their opening four fixtures.

Despite the poor start, John Harris was resolute, and he didn't panic and stuck with his team. Finally, on 3 September, at Craven Cottage, Birchenall gave the Blades their first win of the season.

In the midweek game at home to Spurs, United registered a welcome second victory, Wagstaff and Birchenall scoring the United goals in a 2-1 win. A draw against Everton followed, before a 1-1 draw in the League Cup second round against Sunderland. United won the replay 1-0, with Alan Woodward scoring the winner to book a place in the third round.

On 24 September, United made the short journey across Sheffield to face neighbours Wednesday. United took a two-goal lead through Woodward and Jones, but injuries to skipper

Badger, Bernard Shaw and Birchenall meant United were happy to come home with a point.

Badger, Birchenall and Shaw all missed the next game, at home to West Brom. Cec Coldwell returned in place of Badger, with Munks returning for Shaw. Tom Fenoughty, who had played nine times the previous season, made his first appearance, and replaced Birchenall. The disruption did United no harm and they beat Albion 4-3, Woodward netting twice.

Badger's injury was thought less serious than Birchenall's, and the captain returned to the side against Burnley in round three of the League Cup. United progressed again, winning 2-0. The injury to Badger, though, would keep him out for the next six league games. Coldwell deputised and United were unbeaten in five, winning four and drawing one.

On 5 November 1966, Coldwell started his last game for United, against Sunderland (he was a substitute the following week at Blackpool). He had featured in well over 400 games and had been an integral part of what many consider to be United's greatest ever defence. He announced his retirement from playing aged 37 but stayed at the club he had joined 15 years earlier from Norton Woodseats, as part of the coaching staff.

Unfortunately, the Bonfire Night game at Sunderland was not a happy one, as United were beaten 4-1. Badger and Birchenall returned against Blackpool. The game ended 1-1 but was marred by Reece suffering a broken leg, which kept him out for the rest of the season. Harris signed experienced midfielder Bill Punton from Norwich City as cover.

A week later Birchenall returned to the scoresheet, in another 1-1 draw, this time against Chelsea. United then lost three in a row, including a 3-2 defeat in the League Cup fifth round, at home to Birmingham City. Two draws followed that exit from the cup and extended United's run without a win to five games.

It was possibly surprising then, that over 42,000 were inside the recently improved Bramall Lane for the visit of Manchester United. Birchenall and Jones scored the goals in a 2-1 win, after Herd had levelled for Manchester on the stroke of half-time. As a measure of the merit of that win, the Manchester United side that day included names such as George Best, Denis Law and World Cup winner Bobby Charlton. The Red Devils would go on to win the league by four points.

Back-to-back defeats followed the success over Manchester, but the turn of the year saw an upturn in results. On 7 January 1967, Fulham were thumped 4-0 at Bramall Lane, Jones and Birchenall bagging two each. Defeat at Everton a week later would be the only defeat in nine games, the run coming to an end in the fifth round of the FA Cup. United put Chelsea under pressure and Birchenall saw his effort hit the woodwork, but Chelsea won 2-0 at Stamford Bridge.

Bramall Lane was treated to a 3-3 draw against Aston Villa, with Jones, Birchenall and Woodward all on the mark for United. Three defeats on the bounce followed but Mick Jones scored a first-half winner against Manchester City on April Fool's Day. The home win against City started a sequence of four wins in a row, with the Blades also beating West Ham United, Blackpool and Chelsea. In the closing game of the season, United were beaten 2-0 by Spurs, who were third in the table.

United finished the campaign tenth (one point and one place above the Owls) but there were worrying signs.

The nine-game winless run in the middle of the season

highlighted the frailties in the squad, and there was little doubt that United had suffered as a result of injuries to players such as Gil Reece and Mick Jones.

Chapter 4

IN THE summer of 1967, someone at the club had the bright idea of changing the kit, and United unveiled white shorts for the home strip.

United headed north for pre-season, winning 1-0 at Dundee United. They stayed up north, and on the Tuesday lost 2-0 to Carlisle United. A visit to Carrow Road ended in a 3-1 defeat to Norwich City. A further friendly at Chester finished in a 2-2 draw.

> On 27 August, The Beatles manager, Brian Epstein, was found dead in his London home. The 32-year-old had taken an overdose of sleeping tablets. There has always been, and still is, speculation that he took his own life, although the official cause of death was ruled as accidental. On hearing the news, John Lennon said, 'Our meditations have given us the strength to deal with such a shock.' None of the four Beatles attended the funeral.

Just short of 30,000 fans turned up at Bramall Lane, for the campaign opener against Nottingham Forest, which United lost 1-3. Mick Jones scored his first goal of the season for the Blades.

Two consecutive draws followed, but Reece, returning from the injury that had kept him out for most of the previous season, netted in both games. United won their first game of the season at home to Stoke City, Mick Jones again the scorer in the 1-0 victory.

United then lost five games successively, starting with a 1-0 defeat against Wednesday and ending in a 2-5 mauling by Manchester City. United were knocked out of the League Cup during that sequence and found themselves bottom of the league.

Mick Jones had scored four goals in eight games, and the news that United had accepted an offer for him from Don Revie at Leeds United shocked the fans. The £100,000 Leeds paid for him, however, would put some much-needed money back in the coffers.

Attendances had understandably dropped with the run of defeats and poor form. The home loss to Arsenal in early September was watched by less than 15,000. John Harris shared the fans' anger, and the papers reported that he had resigned but had been persuaded to change his mind.

Mick Jones scored his last goal in a United shirt in that Arsenal game, Alan Birchenall scoring the other, in a 4-2 defeat. Jones was Leeds United's first ever £100,000 signing. He went on to form another fearsome partnership, this time with Allan Clarke. In 1972 Leeds won the FA Cup and, despite dislocating his shoulder during the game, Jones insisted on climbing the famous Wembley steps to collect his winner's medal, with a bandage holding him together. The three England caps he won are not a true reflection of his success.

In his 149 games in a Blades shirt, he scored 63 goals. He scored a further 111 for Leeds. In his final season at Leeds, he was absent for the whole campaign with knee problems. He retired at the age of 30. He played his entire career in the First Division.

Following Jones's departure, Birchenall scored again in the League Cup defeat away at Millwall. United would now need to rely on Birchenall's goals. Three days after the defeat at Millwall, United were beaten 5-2 away at Maine Road.

United finally achieved a second win of the season on 23 September. New signing, Willie Carlin, bought from Carlisle United for £40,000 to replace Jones, scored on his debut, and Reece scored a second in a 2-1 win at home to Newcastle United.

> At the start of October, Che Guevara was reportedly shot dead during a battle in the Bolivian jungle. An examination of the former right-hand man to Fidel Castro's body, showed that the revolutionary was in fact captured and executed. He remains an iconic figure, seen on many a tee-shirt to this day.

The hapless Blades went another six games without tasting victory again. Four defeats and two draws did nothing to improve their league position. They were now second from bottom.

Just as Blades fans were thinking things couldn't get much worse, John Harris took the bewildering decision to sell Alan Birchenall to Chelsea. The fee made Sheffield United the first ever British team to sell two players in a season for £100,000 each: scant consolation for the fans, who had seen arguably their best two players sold. The Blades fans showed their anger at the club's chairman by singing 'Send Dick Wragg to Vietnam!'

Colin Addison was bought from Arsenal, making his United debut in the first week in December, in a 3-0 defeat at West Ham. The following week, on 9 December, the Blades recorded their fourth win of the season, narrowly beating Burnley 1-0.

A fifth win of the campaign came two days before Christmas, Addison scoring his first for the club and Alan Woodward scoring the second in a 2-0 triumph over Coventry City. A 3-3 draw followed on Boxing Day, Wagstaff, Reece, and Woodward all scoring in a thrilling second half, after being 2-0 down at the break.

The last game of 1967 was at home to Southampton, and Addison added two more to the one he scored against Coventry. Woodward added a fourth in a 4-1 home win.

United fans could have been forgiven for fearing the worst heading into the derby with Wednesday on 6 January. It ended 1-1. Rather than the result rallying the troops though, United's league form remained indifferent. A draw at Arsenal preceded a 0-3 scoreline at home to Manchester City.

United's FA Cup fortunes were better, as they beat Watford 1-0 in the third round, then Blackpool 2-1 in round four. However, in between they lost 1-0 at St James' Park against Newcastle United in the league.

United signed promising young forward Tony Currie from third-tier Watford for £26,500. Apparently, Currie was spotted by United scouts when they visited Watford to watch Stewart Scullion and Keith Eddy, and they came back with Currie instead.

He had spent three years with Watford – the first two as an apprentice, after being released by Chelsea. In his first season in the Watford side Currie had scored nine goals in his first 18 games. There was no doubting the teenager's ability, but he was not yet the finished article.

Tony Currie made his Sheffield United debut against Tottenham Hotspur at Bramall Lane on 26 February 1968. He immediately endeared himself to the home crowd by scoring in a greatly entertaining 3-2 victory over Spurs.

> Currie missed the next two games to get married. He was absent for a 1-0 defeat and the FA Cup fifth-round win over West Ham United, Phil Cliff scoring both goals. Cliff scored again when Currie returned to the side against Fulham; the Blades won 1-0.

United had now picked up a few wins but were still struggling to put together a decent run of positive results. Defeat at Sunderland was followed by a 3-1 win at Wolves. They were knocked out of the FA Cup at the quarter-final stage by Leeds United. Leeds would lose to Everton in the semi-finals.

The Blades travelled to Anfield on 12 April, desperately needing a win against a Bill Shankly team that included greats such as Ian St John, Emlyn Hughes and Roger Hunt. United came away victorious, after goals from Currie and Reece.

The next game was against the other Merseyside team, Everton, who beat United 1-0, heaping the pressure back on again. A further defeat at Old Trafford left United desperately needing to find some consistency to escape the drop. Three of their last four fixtures were at home, so there was at least a glimmer of hope for the Blades.

They faced an already relegated Fulham side on Tuesday, 23 April. On the day the new decimal 5p coin came into circulation, Bramall Lane witnessed a five-goal thriller. The Blades led at half-time through Fenoughty. Woodward added a second after the break but United then managed to surrender the two-goal lead and Fulham ran out 2-3 winners. Defeat at home to West Ham United all but confirmed relegation.

United earned a surprise 0-2 win at Burnley, with goals from Currie and Reece, leaving them needing a win on the last day, against Chelsea at Bramall Lane, to survive. Coventry City were also struggling, and defeat for them would mean United could escape the drop with a win. Coventry hadn't won in four games. Wednesday were also in the mix, after not winning a game in nine.

Chelsea had won three of their last four games and sat comfortably in the top half of the table, pushing for a sixth-place finish if they could beat United. If United won, Chelsea's rivals Spurs would grab sixth, as long as they won too. As far as Blades fans were concerned, United needed to win and Coventry had to lose.

United took the lead in the first half through Mick Hill, and at half-time with Coventry level at 0-0, United just needed to keep hold of their slim lead. In the second half though, Chelsea levelled, breaking United's spirit, then broke their hearts by scoring a second.

The unthinkable had happened – Sheffield United and their team of promising young talented footballers were relegated. They finished 23rd in the table, five points above Fulham, but crucially, one point behind Coventry City, who finished their final game 0-0. United had won just 11 games all season. They conceded over 100 goals.

Chapter 5

FOLLOWING RELEGATION, John Harris suggested to the board that he was no longer the right man to lead the team, and that he should move 'upstairs', allowing him to focus on finding, recruiting and coaching new talent for the club.

He accepted responsibility for the club gaining just one point in the last six home games, in front of the new Bramall Lane end. He blamed relegation on his decision to keep hold of players for too long, saying some local players had got into a rut. Many fans believed the fault lay squarely with the sale of talented duo Mick Jones and Alan Birchenall.

Harris told the board that his assistant Andy Beattie should be made manager. Beattie had already managed several clubs including Carlisle United and had briefly been the manager of his native Scotland's national side, albeit on a part-time basis, while he was manager of Huddersfield. He took Scotland to the 1954 World Cup but resigned part way through the tournament due to restrictions placed on him by the Scottish FA. United had approached him to be assistant after Harris had suggested bringing former United legend Jimmy Hagan back to the club in that role.

The board ignored Harris's advice once again, accepting his proposal to move upstairs but rather than put Beattie in charge, United opted for Arthur Rowley instead. Rowley had been a prolific striker during the 1950s and early '60s. His brother Jack played for Manchester United, and Arthur started his career at West Bromwich Albion in 1946, after the war. He moved to Fulham in 1948, where he scored an impressive 19 goals in 22 games, helping Fulham to the Division Two title. His former club, West Brom, finished second. From 1950 he spent eight years at Leicester City, scoring 251 goals in 303 games.

In 1956/57, he scored a fantastic 44 goals in 42 games, securing the title for Leicester City by seven points over Midland rivals Nottingham Forest. In 1958, aged 31, he took the brave step of moving to Shrewsbury Town. Shrewsbury had finished 17th the previous season in the old Third Division South. He is credited with saying on his arrival at Gay Meadow, 'I'd rather win 5-4 than 1-0'.

In Shrewsbury's first season in the newly formed Fourth Division, Rowley scored 38 times in 42 games as player-manager. The Salop fans nicknamed him 'Gunner', due to the awesome power in his left-footed shot. At less than 6ft but over 13 stones in weight, he was a formidable opponent at that level. In the following four seasons he scored 32, 28, 23 and 24 goals respectively, before finally retiring in 1965 ending a playing career of 619 games and 434 goals. His tally should have been 435. On one occasion he had a goal ruled out because he hit the shot – a penalty – so hard, it went through the netting. The referee thought it had gone wide and disallowed the goal.

Rowley remained as manager at Shrewsbury Town, until Dick Wragg, chairman of Sheffield United, approached him to take over the reins from Harris. On 11 July 1968, Arthur Rowley was named manager of newly relegated Sheffield United. Harris made the move upstairs and took the title of general manager.

Rowley set about the task of reshaping and reviving United with vigour. He quickly raided his former club, Shrewsbury Town, and signed versatile midfielder-cum-defender Ted Hemsley for £27,500 and centre-back Eddie Colquhoun from West Bromwich Albion for the same fee. Centre-back Colquhoun had spent the first five years of his career at Bury, where he played 81 games, scoring twice. From Bury, he moved to Jimmy Hagan's West Bromwich Albion.

Rowley also brought in Welsh international defender David Powell from Wrexham. Powell had been an apprentice at Wrexham, where one of his duties was to help the ground staff. He was part of the Wales international set-up at under-23 level and had just broken into the senior squad when Rowley acquired his services. By that time, he had made 134 appearances for Wrexham.

Rowley apparently listened to Harris's comments about keeping players too long as well, as he sold Willie Carlin to Derby County in August, despite the former Liverpool youth player having signed a five-year contract 12 months earlier. Soon afterwards, Ken Mallender was sold to Norwich City.

Preparation for the Second Division started at the unlikely venue of Vale Park, Stoke-on-Trent. Port Vale were Rowley's first opponents in a pre-season friendly that finished 0-3 to the Blades. United then travelled to Holland, as they often had under Harris. The first game ended in defeat at Dos, 1-0. AZ67 were the opposition in the next match, which United won 1-2.

CHAPTER 5

The Second Division campaign got under way at home to Aston Villa. United led 3-0 by half-time, with goals from Woodward, Hill and Currie. Villa pulled one back after the break, but United held on and won 3-1.

Colin Addison scored from the spot in United's first away game, a 1-1 draw at Bristol City. That was the first of four goals in as many games for Addison, who netted in three victories against Derby County, Millwall and Fulham respectively.

United were unbeaten in their opening five games.

Willie Carlin's last game was the Millwall fixture. He moved to Brian Clough's Derby County, where he played an important role in their Division Two title-winning team. Clough later described him as a belligerent, aggressive little Scouser.

For the Fulham match, Carlin was replaced in United's line-up by Frank Barlow. He struggled to get a regular place in the side until much later in the season, though. Mick Hill replaced Barlow in the next game, against Bolton Wanderers, and found himself on the scoresheet; however, United were beaten 4-2, their first defeat of the season.

United suffered their second defeat a week later, in the League Cup at Liverpool. The Reds were convincing 4-0 winners that day. A third consecutive defeat followed, 2-0 away at Norwich City. The honeymoon was over for Rowley.

New signing Ted Hemsley was not at his best in the opening games and was replaced by Wagstaff against Oxford United. Alan Woodward gave the Blades the lead, but two second-half goals from Oxford consigned United to their fourth defeat in a row.

They eventually won again, against Blackpool. Gil Reece and Colin Addison scored the goals that ended a run of seven games without a win. But, United then went another four games without success. Back-to-back draws were followed by back-to-back defeats.

Hemsley returned to the side for the home game with Charlton Athletic and scored his first goal for the team in a 2-0 win. Hemsley had signed for Shrewsbury Town as a schoolboy, under Arthur Rowley's leadership, when he was plucked from a geography lesson and told to 'Go home and get your boots, you're playing tonight.'

He managed to combine his role playing football with also playing first class cricket for Worcestershire. Rowley had supported this, and Shrewsbury always accommodated it. He played for his county for 21 years, scoring almost 10,000 runs, including eight centuries, and 53 half-centuries. In one well-documented innings, he scored 176 not out. When asked if he was a footballing cricketer or a cricketing footballer, Hemsley insists he was both. 'I came from a mining village in South Shropshire and in those days the coal board made sure – as they did all around the country – that the village had a recreation ground; so we had two football pitches, a bowling green, youth club, cricket pitches, tennis courts, and so on. I played everything on that recreation ground. I loved sports.'

If Ted Hemsley could have found time to be a professional tennis player as well as a professional footballer and cricketer, I'm sure he would have done.

In those days, of course, cricket was still played regularly at Bramall Lane; indeed the football ground was then three-sided, with a pavilion on the south side. Hemsley had the distinction of playing cricket for Worcestershire against Yorkshire at Bramall Lane. He remembers walking out of the old pavilion to a chorus of slow hand-claps, only to realise it was his United team-mates. As he walked through the gate to enter the field, Fred Trueman told him, 'Dunt bother shuttin' t' gate lad, tha'll be going back through it in a minute.'

Rowley's other new signing, Eddie Colquhoun, scored his first goal for United a week after the Charlton game in a 2-1 defeat at Portsmouth. Colquhoun had made his debut against Huddersfield Town away, and Rowley named him captain for his home debut, in the win over Charlton Athletic.

It was mid-November before United managed consecutive wins again. John Tudor scored a brace on his home debut in the 2-0 win over Bury, and repeated the trick the following week against Preston in a 4-2 victory. Tudor had been bought from Coventry City, where he had been less than prolific – scoring 13 in 69 games. Now he had scored four in two games for the Blades.

The winning run of two games was halted before it could gain any momentum though and the Blades went down 1-4 to Cardiff City at the end of November. Hemsley scored his second for the club on 8 December in a 2-0 win over Birmingham City, Alan Woodward scoring the other. The remaining two games of December finished in draws.

On 2 January, Rupert Murdoch gained control of the News of the World group. A £34m bid from rival Robert Maxwell's Pergamon Press was beaten by the 37-year-old, who already owned a paper in his native Australia. Murdoch's business empire would go from strength to strength, and he would go on to form BSkyB in 1990 and be CEO of 21st Century Fox. He is one of the most powerful men in the world, and in 2016 he remarkably married Mick Jagger's ex-wife Jerry Hall, who is almost 30 years his junior. His net worth is just short of $22billion.

John Tudor scored again as United were knocked out of the FA Cup, in the third round against Third Division Mansfield Town in early January. United were firm favourites for the tie, and took thousands of expectant fans to Field Mill, the attendance bulging at 17,430. In pre-health-and-safety days, there was little more than a length of string separating the opposing fans, who saw Dudley Roberts score twice for Mansfield as the hosts beat United 2-1. It could have been seen as a total embarrassment, but for the antics of the Stags later in the competition.

Mansfield Town would overcome Southend United in the next round and were drawn against First Division West Ham United in the fifth round. The Stags sat just above the relegation zone on goal difference when they faced the Hammers. The game had been postponed five times, in which time Ron Greenwood's West Ham were on a seven-game winless run in the league. There were even more fans inside Field Mill than there had been when they beat United; 21,117 were packed inside to watch the spectacle. After just over 20 minutes, Mansfield took the lead through Dudley Roberts and by half-time they led 2-0. The dreadful pitch at Mansfield did not assist West Ham's First Division players and Mansfield beat Bobby Moore's men 3-0 in a famous victory, which outshone the win over United. They would face Leicester in the quarter-finals, and when the tie was postponed, Mansfield Town were included in the semi-final draw for the first time in their history. Unfortunately for them, they were beaten 0-1 by Leicester and never made it past the quarters.

Woodward scored twice in United's win at Portsmouth on 11 January and Tudor scored the winner at Carlisle United, taking his tally to six. United then won just once in their next five outings, a 5-0 thrashing of Bury, in which Tudor scored a hat-trick. Form remained erratic for the rest of the season.

United finished a disappointing ninth in Division Two. Tudor scored 16 goals in 24 appearances in all competitions, more than he had scored in 69 outings for his previous club, Coventry City. Eddie Colquhoun quickly established himself in the side, and his rugged, no-nonsense approach meant he soon became a favourite with the crowd. His popularity prompted the song from the Bramall Lane crowd, 'Ain't got a barrel of money, but we've got Woodward and Currie, with Eddie Colquhoun, promotion is soon, United.'

The consensus was that Rowley had done reasonably well in the transfer market. At the end of the season, he sold both the Wagstaff brothers to Reading, Bernard Shaw to Wolves and Munks to Portsmouth. He signed defender John Flynn from Workington for £5,000 after he was spotted by now general manager, John Harris.

Pre-season got under way at Haarlem in Holland, with a 0-0 draw. Another draw followed, this time in West Germany against VFL Bochum, which ended 1-1. Back in Holland for the third warm-up, United won 3-0 against De Graafschap, before drawing again at Elinkwijk, John Tudor and Tony Currie both on target for the Blades. A final pre-season workout against Walsall away saw yet another draw, this time 1-1 with Currie the scorer again.

It had not been the most inspiring of preparations and United fans were becoming unhappy with Rowley. There was a feeling amongst some fans that Rowley wasn't present or committed enough, and whether there is any truth to the suggestion or not, some fans thought he would rather be at the racetrack.

On 6 August 1969, just three days before the opening game of the 1969/70 season, Arthur Rowley was sacked. He went on to be manager of Southend United and remained popular at Shrewsbury Town, the team he had played for and managed before coming to Bramall Lane. In 2000, Shrewsbury fans named him as their greatest ever player. At their ground even today, there is an Arthur Rowley Suite, available for functions.

Most United fans, however, have few fond memories of his one season in charge. Most of the players, though, thought that the club let him go too soon.

John Harris made the move back downstairs and was reinstated as manager.

Chapter 6

THE SECOND coming of John Harris began with a convincing 3-0 thrashing of Middlesbrough. Boro' had finished fourth the previous season but were no match for the revitalised Blades. Reece opened the scoring and Woodward got the other two. Ted Hemsley, who had featured in all the pre-season games under Rowley, was left out by Harris.

United won their opening three league games under Harris, with Alan Woodward and Tony Currie both in good form. Woodward scored four in those three games and Currie scored three.

United's first defeat of the 1969/70 campaign came in the Tuesday night trip to Charlton Athletic. Tudor and Reece scored for the Blades, but Charlton won 3-2. United then went on a five-match unbeaten run, winning four and drawing one before losing for the second time, away at Birmingham City on 13 September. A midweek goalless draw with Oxford United preceded another win at home to Cardiff City – Reece scoring the winner against his home-town club.

The Blades then progressed to the fourth round of the League Cup, beating Luton Town 3-0, and then lost away at

Preston North End. United's home form was excellent, and it would be mid-October before they suffered defeat at Bramall Lane, beaten 2-3 by Blackpool. Away form was less impressive though, and United lost for the fourth successive game on the road, at Millwall's Den. Hemsley returned to the United line-up following the loss at Millwall.

Decent home form continued and on 1 November, United spanked Blackburn Rovers 4-0. Currie, Addison and Woodward scored, and even Len Badger grabbed one.

Two away games followed, without success – at Queens Park Rangers and Bolton Wanderers – before another home masterclass. Eddie Colquhoun scored twice, Reece snatched one, Powell converted a penalty and Currie added a fifth against Aston Villa. Alan Woodward then scored the winner in a rare away victory at Carlisle United.

In early December, the Blades were rampant again at the Lane, putting six past Birmingham City without reply. Despite being unbeaten at Bramall Lane all season, crowds were still not growing and just over 17,000 watched Colin Addison score two of the six. United had now scored 13 goals in four games, without conceding.

The second half of December was less productive. Following the thrashing of Birmingham City, the Blades drew 1-1 at Norwich City, then lost away at Huddersfield Town on Boxing Day.

At the turn of the decade, in the FA Cup third round, United were drawn against First Division Everton at home. The away side took the lead, then United rattled the woodwork several times before two flying headers from Reece and Addison sealed the win for them. United deserved the victory, outplaying an Everton side that went on to win the league title that year, losing just three games all season. A week later United lost 3-0 away at Cardiff City, despite fielding exactly the same starting XI as the one that had beaten top-flight Everton.

They bounced back at home to Preston North End, winning 2-0 before facing Derby County away in the fourth round of the FA Cup on 24 January. From 2-0 down at the interval, United were unable to turn the game around, as they had in the previous round at home, and slipped out of the competition after the game finished 3-0.

Alan Woodward, Tony Currie and Eddie Colquhoun were all playing superbly, and all three of them scored for the Blades in wins in February, but March was poor. After beating Carlisle United 1-0 at home, four defeats in a row ensued, with United only managing to find the net once.

After losing to Blackpool on the Monday night, the Blades beat Millwall 3-1 on the Tuesday, goals from Tudor, Currie and Woodward securing the win. Colquhoun scored the only goal against Bristol a week later.

A five-goal crescendo ensured a sixth-place finish for United as Tudor, Reece, Woodward (two) and Currie all found the net at home to Oxford United.

Second-placed Blackpool finished just four points ahead of United. Were it not for the disastrous run in March, United could have finished much higher and possibly gained promotion, although runaway champions Huddersfield Town finished top of the table by seven clear points.

United supporters were disappointed by the season, notwithstanding the fantastic FA Cup win over Everton. The fans would not be consoled by the signing of 26-year-old Bill Dearden from Fourth Division Chester. Dearden had started out at Oldham Athletic, before helping Crewe Alexandra win promotion from the Fourth Division in 1967/68. From Crewe he had moved to Chester where he scored 22 goals in 85 games.

Dearden signed for the Blades in August 1970, for a relatively small fee of £10,000, possibly because he was known to have cartilage issues.

United also signed 31-year-old John Barnwell from Nottingham Forest for £20,000. Barnwell had started promisingly at Arsenal. He played for the Gunners at youth level and achieved England youth and under-23 caps before being called up for national service. In 1964 he joined Nottingham Forest, where he played as a defensive midfielder, scoring 22 goals in 186 games over six years, but had a persistent ankle problem.

Barnwell made his Sheffield United debut in a pre-season friendly away at Swansea City. United won 3-2 with two goals from Alan Woodward and one from Gil Reece. Barnwell started again in a second friendly, this time away at Millmoor against Rotherham United, Currie and Colquhoun scoring in a 2-0 win.

In Barnwell's league debut for United, the Blades suffered a hangover from the poor away form of the previous season, and lost the season opener 3-1 at Orient.

Bill Dearden made his debut in United's first home game of the season, a 2-1 win over Swindon Town. A 0-1 defeat at Norwich City preceded a 1-1 draw at Cardiff City.

United's second home game of the 1970/71 season saw an exciting 3-3 draw with Bristol City. Alan Woodward scored his third of the season with an unstoppable shot and Bill Dearden scored a second for the Blades, before substitute John Tudor scored his first of the season, drawing them level in the last minute, after the away side had led 0-3.

On 8 September, Tony Currie scored the winner with a fine shot in the League Cup second round against First Division Leeds United. It was a fantastic result against a Leeds side that finished the season second in the league, narrowly beaten by Arsenal, but 12 points above third-placed Spurs.

> Rock star Jimi Hendrix collapsed and died after a party in London, on 18 September 1970. The 27-year-old had transformed electric guitar playing, occasionally using his teeth or chain saws instead of a plectrum. An open verdict was recorded on Hendrix's death, with the coroner saying there was no evidence of drug addiction, despite Hendrix having taken nine sleeping tablets before his collapse. In 2003 Hendrix was voted the best ever rock guitarist by *Rolling Stone* Magazine. At the time of his death, he was thought to be worth $500,000.

Tony Currie scored again in an away win at Millwall, and Bill Dearden scored his second for his new club in a 1-1 draw with Middlesbrough. At the end of September, the fabulous Alan Woodward scored a hat-trick in a 5-1 away win at Portsmouth.

On 3 October, Sheffield United met Sheffield Wednesday, who had just been relegated from the First Division. Almost 40,000 watched the derby match. Eddie Colquhoun scored inside six minutes with a header from a Woodward free kick. Five minutes later Dearden got on the end of a Woodward cross to make it 2-0. Wednesday levelled with goals from Tommy Craig and Jack Sinclair in the second half before Tudor, on as a substitute for Gil Reece, nutmegged Owls keeper Peter Grummitt to secure the 3-2 victory for United.

United were then defeated in the League Cup third round at Spurs, Ted Hemsley getting the consolation in a 1-2 loss.

A nine-match unbeaten league run followed through October and November. After beating Birmingham City1-0 and Leyton Orient 3-1, United drew three games before winning 3-1 at Blackburn Rovers and then drawing another two. It would be 5 December before United did finally lose, 2-1 away at Luton Town.

A run of patchy form then saw United beat Charlton Athletic 3-0, but lose by the same scoreline at Swindon Town. On Boxing Day, United beat Leicester City 2-1 at the Lane and the Blades went out of the FA Cup in the third round, losing 2-0 to Portsmouth on 2 January 1971.

At the Old Firm derby on that day, 66 fans lost their lives, while they were leaving Ibrox. The notorious stairway 13 had been under scrutiny before. Ten years earlier, two fans had died when they were crushed in the steep stairwell. In 1967 more fans were injured and again in 1969, when a further 26 fans were hurt. Rangers had spent a significant sum of money trying to improve safety. Although fraught with danger, the exit was a popular one, as it was the one nearest to buses and subways.

Over 80,000 fans were packed into Ibrox when Jimmy Johnson scored for Celtic with just minutes to go and as Rangers fans started to leave early, tragedy struck. Rangers equalised deep in stoppage time, and it was initially thought that as fans tried to rush back into the ground, someone may have fallen resulting in a pile-up of people – however, the inquiry that followed found this theory was untrue.

Among those who lost their lives were 31 teenagers, including one female – 18-year-old Margaret Ferguson – and many younger children. The youngest to perish was just nine years old. Then Rangers manager, Willie Waddell, ensured his players attended the funerals of all those who perished and visited the injured in hospital. Some of those players were themselves just teenagers.

One younger Celtic player, Kenny Dalglish, was present in the stadium that day. Sir Kenny went on to be a Celtic legend, before achieving even greater success with Liverpool. While at Liverpool, Dalglish was in Brussels in May 1985 for the European Cup Final, when the Heysel Stadium tragedy occurred.

An hour before Juventus and Liverpool were due to kick off, trouble erupted in the crowd and 39 fans, mostly Italians, were killed and around 600 others were injured. As a result, English clubs were banned indefinitely by UEFA from all European competitions. The ban wasn't lifted until 1990.

Dalglish completed a terrible treble of tragedies, as he was also present at the Hillsborough disaster, in April 1989, which resulted in the deaths of 94 Liverpool fans on the day, and three more since then.

Back to the 1970/71 season, and United took revenge on Portsmouth for the FA Cup loss, beating them 2-0 in the league a week later. They then lost 2-1 at Bolton Wanderers.

Harris decided he needed to strengthen his side at this point and bought midfielder Trevor Hockey from Birmingham City for £40,000.

Hockey was born in Keighley, North Yorkshire, and started his career at Bradford City, making his debut aged 17. After playing 53 games for the Bantams, he moved to Nottingham

Forest, then Newcastle United, then Birmingham. He played 231 games for Birmingham and was their player of the year in 1969.

His instruction from Harris was to battle, to win the ball, and give it to Tony Currie.

Harris also swapped John Tudor, who had scored nine goals, for David Ford, an ex-Wednesday winger from Newcastle United. Tudor went on to score over 70 goals for Newcastle in seven seasons. He formed a fearsome partnership with Malcolm Macdonald.

He was fondly thought of by the Toon fans and when Tudor's son announced on Christmas Eve, a couple of years ago, that his dad was in poor health due to Alzheimer's, the Newcastle fans paid tribute. During the Boxing Day trip to Anfield, despite their side losing 4-0, the Geordie fans gave a rendition of 'Hallelujah John Tudor'. Tudor, who lives in the USA after moving to Minnesota when his playing career ended, was moved to tears by the gesture.

Sheffield-born Ford had made his debut for Sheffield Wednesday in 1965. He came off the bench in a game against Sunderland to become Wednesday's first ever substitute. He scored 13 goals in 18 league and cup games that season and helped Wednesday reach the FA Cup Final. He scored their second goal during the showpiece match against Everton, to make it 2-0. Sadly though, Everton scored the next three and the Owls lost.

In 1967 Ford was involved in a tragic car accident, which he took a while to recover from, and was eventually sold to Newcastle.

The signing of goalkeeper John Hope ended Alan Hodgkinson's 17 years at United. Hodgkinson had made

576 appearances for the Blades, but his last game came in a friendly at Chesterfield on 23 January 1971, which ended in a 1-0 defeat.

Hodgkinson would go on to have a highly successful coaching career at clubs including Aston Villa, Rangers, Sheffield Wednesday and both Manchester clubs. He is credited with bringing the magnificent Peter Schmeichel to Manchester United and also worked as Scotland's goalkeeping coach.

Blades fan Geoff Barnsley remembers one occasion, standing on the railings at the Bramall Lane end. He handed Hodgkinson the ball and touched his Brylcreemed hair as the great keeper said, 'Hurry up, we're losing.'

Hope had started at Darlington before moving to Newcastle, but only played for them once – as cover for Willie McFaul. It would be a big step for Hope going from understudy to filling the gloves of Hodgkinson.

Tony Currie's superb form earned him an England under-23 call-up, and on 24 February 1971 he scored the equaliser against Scotland, making it 2-2.

Hope, Hockey and Ford made their debuts in a 2-1 win away at Oxford United, which saw Dearden bag a brace in the first of four consecutive wins. A 0-1 defeat at Carlisle, and a 1-2 loss at home to Hull on 9 March would be United's last defeats of the season.

The Blades drew 2-2 with Queens Park Rangers away, then hammered Blackburn Rovers 5-0 at Bramall Lane. David Ford scored his first for United, Woodward, Reece, Colquhoun and Dearden got the other four.

Currie scored a first-half winner at Bristol City before United drew the next three games 0-0, including the return fixture at Hillsborough.

Trevor Hockey scored his first United goal in a 2-0 win over Millwall. Hockey showed plenty of the drive and determination in midfield that he had been bought for, by scoring while falling over and quickly endearing himself to the fans.

Charles Manson and three members of his cult were sentenced to death in the USA, in March 1971. They were found guilty of eight murders that had taken place in 1969 in California, including that of actress Sharon Tate, who was heavily pregnant, and her unborn child. Manson was ejected from court proceedings after telling the judge that he had no authority, and was not nearly as good as Manson. The accused all admitted the killings while under the influence of LSD. The case was one of the longest in history, and before the evil killers could be put down, the death penalty was abolished in California, and the four were sentenced to life in prison instead (even though capital punishment was later allowed once more). Manson was denied parole more than ten times and remained in prison until his death in 2017.

In United's next game, against Birmingham City, Gil Reece played brilliantly and scored twice. Alan Woodward added a third.

Dearden scored a bullet header from a Tony Currie cross to salvage a point away at Middlesbrough, before a promotion-chasing Cardiff City, who were a point behind United but had a game in hand, came to Bramall Lane on Tuesday, 27 April. They were overwhelmed by a resplendent Sheffield United team. Dearden scored twice and Flynn, Currie and Reece scored one each in a 5-1 rout at Bramall Lane in front of 42,963 fans.

United finally clinched promotion back to the First Division in the final game of the season, at home to Watford on 1 May, ten years after they were last promoted. Woodward scored from 12 yards and Gil Reece scored twice in a 3-0 win to prompt celebrations.

United had lost just once at Bramall Lane all season.

Blades fan Kevin Gascoigne remembers this being the season when he fell in love with United. He mused, 'John Harris produced an amazing team. I was only 11, and we used to go to the Ball Inn training ground on Myrtle Road, every day during the school holidays, to watch the team train.

'I remember Trevor Hockey's purple velvet car and the boys were so friendly with us. The last few weeks of the season, especially the Cardiff game that was a must-win, will live with me forever.'

Division Two table 1970/71

	Played	*W*	*D*	*L*	*Points*
1 Leicester City	42	23	13	6	59
2 **Sheffield United**	42	21	14	7	56

Chapter 7

TO CELEBRATE promotion, United unveiled plans to build a new South Stand where the cricket pavilion stood. It was an ambitious scheme, that would leave very little money to strengthen the team.

Winger Stewart Scullion, from Watford, would be the only signing John Harris made for United's return to the First Division. He had initially watched him in 1968, before buying Currie instead. Scullion had turned professional at Charlton Athletic but never played a game for them. He was bought by Watford manager Ken Furphy in 1966 and subsequently helped the Hornets to promotion. Harris paid £25,000 for him.

After a win and two defeats abroad, United completed pre-season by welcoming neighbours Wednesday to the Lane. A crowd of 17,500 (which wasn't many, even for a Monday night friendly) watched a 2-2 draw. Tony Currie and Alan Woodward scored for the Blades.

The 1971/72 season – the eagerly awaited return to the top flight of English football – started at home to Southampton on 14 August. The headline on the front of the matchday programme pronounced, 'It's great to be back!' Woodward scored a penalty and Geoff Salmons and John Flynn added two more, beating the Saints 3-1.

> Also in the news that weekend was show jumper Harvey Smith. Smith lost his £2,000 winnings and the British Show Jumping Derby for sticking two fingers up at the judges after an almost perfect round. Yorkshireman Smith claimed the gesture meant V for victory, and subsequently had the decision reversed two days later.

On 17 August, United beat the 1969 league champions, Leeds United 3-0, Flynn, Dearden and Colquhoun scoring in front of over 40,000 inside Bramall Lane. Four days later Alan Woodward scored the only goal in a 1-0 win at Goodison Park over 1970 FA Cup semi-finalists, Everton.

United rounded off an incredible treble by beating 1970/71 champions, Arsenal, 1-0 at Highbury, winger Scullion scoring his first goal for the Blades. It really was great to be back!

The winning start stuttered at home to West Bromwich Albion as the sides drew 0-0. Three more wins, two in the league and one in the League Cup second round, followed: 3-1 over Huddersfield Town, 2-3 over Nottingham Forest, and 3-0 over Fulham in the cup. Billy Dearden scored in all three games.

Dearden scored another in the 2-2 draw with Spurs on 11 September. On 18 September, against Leicester City, Currie and Salmons linked up well to earn a corner late on, Salmons running past three defenders before his shot was turned around the post by Peter Shilton. Woodward took the ensuing corner, curling it directly into the net with five minutes remaining: 1-0, United.

Unbeaten in 22 games, a run that extended back to March the previous season, United sat proudly at the top of the Football League after winning eight of their opening ten matches. Manchester United were sitting in second place, three points behind the Blades, when United travelled to Old Trafford on 2 October.

With the game in the balance, George Best ran at the Sheffield defence, past three defenders, before curling a low shot into the far corner, in a goal that is often shown on TV as one of the brilliant Irishman's best. Len Badger tried in vain to make a last-gasp save but as he slid into the back of the net, the ball was already nestling in it and Best was wheeling away to celebrate. Manchester United won 2-0.

Sheffield United then progressed through round three of the League Cup, by beating York City 3-2. In a disappointing October, the Blades lost three in a row, against Stoke City, Southampton and Manchester City, and drew 0-0 with Arsenal in the fourth round of the League Cup.

Injuries and suspensions would prove costly to United's small squad and as Harris was forced to change his team, form began to suffer.

Tony Currie scored what he later described as one of his finest goals, against Liverpool in a 1-1 draw at home. Picking the ball up in midfield he lifted it into the far corner, past a helpless Ray Clemence from about 40 yards. The commentator on TV quipped, 'You'd have to go through a whole season to see a better goal than that,' as Currie blew kisses to the adoring crowd.

Gil Reece then scored both goals in a 2-1 win against West Ham United. Two days later Reece scored again, in a 2-0 League Cup fourth-round replay victory over Arsenal after Alan Woodward had given United the lead.

Woodward netted twice in a 2-0 win at Bramall Lane against Coventry City on 13 November. Four days later, in the fifth round of the League Cup, against West Ham – the team United had beaten less than a fortnight earlier – the match finished as a 5-0 defeat. Brian 'Pop' Robson scored a hat-trick past a poor Hope.

Away from home, against Derby County, Ted Hemsley was judged to have handled, and hurled the ball at the referee when a penalty was awarded. Len Badger was booked for his protests while Hemsley escaped punishment, but the Rams converted their second penalty of the match to make it 3-0.

Ipswich Town came to the Lane on 27 November. In a superb first half, United were leading 4-0 by the break and ended up grabbing seven without reply. Alan Woodward scored four; Reece, Badger and Dearden also got on the scoresheet. Len Badger's goal was one of his most memorable, and one that is embedded in United folklore. Some fans recall him hitting it from the halfway line into the top corner, others remember it being even further out. Some say it was a lob, other call it a pile-driver. Whatever it was, it wrapped up a superb victory.

Bill Dearden scored again against Crystal Palace in early December, but this time the Blades were on the other end of a hiding, losing 5-1.

The Blades boss characteristically refused to panic and named an unchanged team to face Wolves the following week, showing his belief in his players. United were two down by the break but Woodward and Currie scored second-half goals to pull United level.

Ian Mackenzie came in for John Flynn against Nottingham Forest, and Alan Woodward and Tony Currie were on target again for the Blades as they beat Forest 2-1.

Tony Currie found the net for the third time in as many games at St James' Park two days after Christmas. United beat Newcastle 1-2, Scullion with the other goal in front of a crowd of 53,000.

> January didn't start well, either in Sheffield or the rest of Britain; the miners went on strike on the ninth day of the new year. They walked out in the first national strike for 50 years as 280,000 workers withdrew their labour in a fight for a £9 per week pay rise. On 5 January, the national executive committee of the NUM rejected a pay offer from the National Coal Board, who then withdrew all pay offers. By the end of the month one million people were unemployed in the UK for the first time since the 1930s. British Steel had announced redundancies leading to 1,300 job losses and 2,000 dock workers lost their jobs. In February a four-day working week was introduced to save electricity as a national state of emergency was declared.

There was little to lift the gloom in football either. Two draws against Leicester City and West Brom, in which Dearden scored in each, were followed by an exit from the FA Cup in a third-round defeat at home to Cardiff City.

United then lost 0-1 at Leeds United and 0-5 at home to Arsenal. The great Charlie George scored two. To add insult to injury, midfielder Alan Ball famously and audaciously sat on the ball during the game.

In early February, the Blades played two friendlies. The first was at Jaffa against an Israel XI, and then United hosted Dynamo Kiev at the Lane, losing 1-2. Tom McAlister played in goal for both games, and Mick Speight appeared as a substitute in the latter.

Against Manchester City on 12 February, United fought back from two down. Bill Dearden pulled one back then Alan Woodward levelled from the spot before Currie headed in a Woodward corner to make it 2-3. However, midfielder Mick Speight, making his home debut in front of 30,000 fans, made a fine save on the line, after Hope was beaten, when the ball stuck in the mud. The resulting penalty was converted to make it 3-3. Influential midfielder Trevor Hockey broke his leg in the game.

Speight explains, 'It was difficult to break into this quality side, but once you arrived it was a great education of football. Learning by doing is the best way to learn. All of the team were supportive. It was easy to play alongside such quality, but you were expected to give something to the team as well. They were all my best friends but if you couldn't play at that level, you soon got found out. It was every boy's dream though. A full house against a top side.'

A week later United travelled to Anfield to play Liverpool and were beaten 2-0. Speight kept his place. Despite the defeat, Speight recalls the occasion fondly, 'It was a fantastic feeling, Anfield full, in front of their famous Kop and against so many international players, was just amazing. My learning under John Harris between 1968 and '72 was a great education, learning the game from the inside – working and playing with great players was fantastic.'

The miners' strike was now in its sixth week and all 289 pits in England and Wales remained closed. Many households across the country faced having no electricity for up to nine hours a day. The electricity shortage meant many businesses faced closure and unemployment was already up to 1.2 million as the UK lurched into darkness.

On 29 February Billy Dearden lit up Bramall Lane when he scored a hat-trick to beat West Ham 3-0 and take some revenge for the mauling in the cup earlier in the season.

'They called it the perfect hat-trick, left foot, right foot, header. And against Bobby Moore,' a gleeful Dearden remembers.

The next game – against Coventry – was abandoned after just over an hour, due to snow and bad light with United two up. The next five games would be marginally more fruitful.

United drew 2-2 with Stoke, and Alan Woodward scored a penalty against Everton to earn a point. A third successive draw at Huddersfield preceded a 2-0 defeat by Spurs. The fifth game without a win came at Stamford Bridge. Currie was absent and Frank Barlow made his final appearance in a Blades shirt as Chelsea won 2-0. Barlow had been at Bramall Lane for seven years, making 121 appearances. Harris would change tactics, as many teams did in those days, when playing away. Barlow featured predominantly in away games but would be left out of the side at home. If you weren't in the first team, you would usually play for the reserves. When the first team played at home, the reserves would play away. Mrs Barlow is thought to have written to John Harris, complaining that her husband was away from home every week – much to the amusement of the other players.

Following his exit from United, Barlow signed for Chesterfield. He played 140 games for them over four seasons, scoring three goals – one more than he scored for United. He enjoyed a brief stint in the North American Soccer League (NASL) for Boston Minutemen, before returning to Saltergate as manager in 1980. He had previously been caretaker when Joe Shaw was sacked and he was made permanent manager following the departure of Arthur Cox.

Always more comfortable as a coach, Barlow was often a reluctant manager. He achieved success in his first season in charge though, leading the Spireites to the Anglo-Scottish Cup Final, where they were crowned champions after beating Notts County 2-1. Following Chesterfield's relegation, new owners came in and fired the entire coaching team, although Barlow was retained. Loyal to his team, he resigned and headed to Scunthorpe as assistant to Allan Clarke. When Clarke later resigned, Frank Barlow reluctantly stepped up again. He remained in post until 1987.

In 2005, new Nottingham Forest manager Gary Megson appointed Barlow as his assistant. When Megson failed to gain success, he left Forest and Barlow once more stepped up to be caretaker manager. Forest were unbeaten in ten games under Barlow and co-caretaker Ian McPartland.

After leaving Forest, and spells as caretaker at Hull, assistant at Bradford and again at Wigan, Danny Wilson named Barlow as his assistant at Bramall Lane. His almost 50 years in the game had brought him full circle, back to his first team – United.

Back to 1972, and on April Fool's Day, United completed the double over Newcastle United, beating them 1-0 at the Lane. On 8 April, 34,212 saw United lose 0-4 to Derby County. A poor goal kick gave the ball away and Archie Gemmill punished it to score the opener. An own goal by Ian

Mackenzie made it 0-2, Kevin Hector headed a third, and John O'Hare added a fourth.

United failed to win their next two matches but won the last two games of the season, at home to Crystal Palace 1-0, and away at Wolves 1-2, with Dearden and Currie scoring for the Blades.

United finished tenth, which all things considered wasn't a bad result for a first season back in the top flight with severely limited resources.

With the new South Stand expected to cost in the region of £650,000, there was little money to buy new players for the 1972/73 season, but Harris somehow managed to bring in midfielder Keith Eddy from Watford.

Eddy had started his career ten years earlier at Barrow but had grown disillusioned at constant transfer rumours, and after not showing up to pre-season was eventually sold to Watford. In 1968/69 they won the Third Division championship together.

Eddie Colquhoun returned from a successful tour with Scotland in Brazil where he played alongside greats such as Billy Bremner, Denis Law and Willie Morgan as the Scots took on Brazil, Czechoslovakia and Yugoslavia.

During pre-season, United took part in the 1972 Watney Cup, a by-invitation tournament between the top-scoring teams of all four divisions, two teams from each. Although short-lived, being contested for just four years, the Watney Cup was one of the first tournaments to be sponsored and shown live on TV. There was prize money involved too: £50,000 from sponsorship money was shared between the Football Association and the Football League, with each side taking £4,000 for competing. Each of the winning first-round teams received an extra £500.

Another £500 went to the victorious semi-finalists, and £1,000 for the outright winners. To give that seemingly low (by today's standards) amount some relevance, the average house in 1972 would cost around £5,000. First Division players could expect to earn in the region of £75 per week (still more than double the average weekly wage).

The tournament was first contested in 1970, and that year's final was between Derby County and Manchester United, ending 4-1 to Derby. The following year Colchester United beat West Brom on penalties. United were involved but lost early in the competition. In 1972, the Blades took part again.

They began the event on 28 July against Notts County, winning 3-0. Alan Woodward opened the scoring with a trademark long-range, right-footed drive from outside the box. Tony Currie added a second after winning the ball with his face and slotting it past the keeper. Currie later added a third with a brilliant swivel volley inside the six-yard box.

On 2 August, away at Peterborough United, Mackenzie nodded the first goal from a flick-on at the near post from Bill Dearden after 17 minutes. Dearden headed a second, then an effortless through-ball from Woodward found Dearden again, who beat his defender before being tripped in the box. Woodward slotted home from the spot. Ted Hemsley beat two men to score a great solo effort to make it 4-0 and put United through to the final, against Third Division Bristol Rovers.

Goalkeeping of the highest order from both keepers (19-year-old Tom McAlister in goal for United and Dick Shepherd for Rovers) ensured a 0-0 draw, sending the final to penalties. McAlister went the wrong way for the first one, tucked neatly away into the corner by Roberts. Alan

Woodward levelled, Shepherd seeming to hurt his hand trying unsuccessfully to keep it out.

Rovers went 2-1 up before new signing Keith Eddy equalised with literally his first kick for the Blades to make it 2-2. Rovers again converted their kick before Tony Currie thumped his penalty straight at Shepherd. Still 3-2, but the referee judged the keeper had moved and ordered the kick to be retaken, no mistake this time, 3-3. Bannister made it 4-3, McAlister going the wrong way again. Dearden converted his kick for 4-4.

Then it was 5-4, McAlister going in the opposite direction to the ball for a fifth time. Captain Eddie Colquhoun smashed his into the roof of the net for 5-5 – sudden death.

McAlister didn't move: 6-5.

Scullion: 6-6.

Beleaguered McAlister was stationary again as Bristol went 7-6 up. Finally, Hemsley's poor penalty was saved by Shepherd. Rovers won 7-6.

The season proper got under way a week later, at Birmingham City's St Andrew's. Trevor Hockey and Alan Woodward scored the goals in a 1-2 win. United then uncharacteristically lost back-to-back home games, against Leeds United on the Tuesday night, and Newcastle United on the Saturday afternoon. Reece scored a brace in a 2-2 draw away at Stoke City's Victoria Ground on the Wednesday night.

A 0-0 draw at home to Ipswich Town on 29 August was United's third home game without a win. It proved fourth time lucky though, and on 2 September 1972, United beat Southampton 3-1. Alan Woodward opened the scoring with a deft touch to turn the defender before lashing the ball home for 1-0. Bill Dearden added a second after Tony Currie intercepted a goal kick and flicked through to Dearden in the box. Southampton pulled one back after a soft header squirmed in, but Dearden added his second of the game, lobbing the advancing keeper brilliantly, to make it 3-1 on the stroke of full time.

> The 1972 summer Olympic Games in Germany were struck by tragedy when 11 Israeli athletes were kidnapped and taken hostage from the Olympic village. Two of the hostages resisted and were killed almost immediately. While the Games continued, the kidnappers demanded 200 Palestinian prisoners being held in Israel be released. The siege ended in a bloody shootout, resulting in all nine athletes being killed. The German government had agreed to pay any price for the athletes to be released and provided three helicopters. As the helicopters landed, a planned ambush went wrong and a gun battle began, which resulted in at least two of the kidnappers and all the remaining hostages being killed. It is widely reported that the Israelis responded by starting a campaign known as Operation Wrath of God, where those thought to be responsible were hunted and killed. In 2005, the events were turned into a film by Steven Spielberg, called *Munich*.

The victory over the Saints would be Gil Reece's last appearance for the Blades before returning to the team he began his career at, Cardiff City – in exchange for Alan Warboys. Reece had made over 200 appearances for United and was considered by many fans to be the best header of a ball ever to don the red and white stripes.

He played 100 games for the Bluebirds, scoring 23 goals and being given the club captaincy. His goals helped Cardiff win the Welsh Cup; he scored a hat-trick in the second leg of the 1973 final. Reece won 29 international caps for Wales – the last coming in 1975 against Northern Ireland. He might have won more caps, but en route to a World Cup qualifier against East Germany, in 1969, it emerged that the Welsh FA had not booked enough tickets for the flight. As they were forced to select the squad in alphabetical order, Reece missed out.

When his pro career ended, he turned out for non-league Barry Town, before starting a heating business. In 2000, after suffering a series of cysts in his right knee, he was forced to have the leg removed. He passed away three years later, aged 61.

At home to Chelsea on 16 September, a Tony Currie throw to Alan Woodward was lobbed first time into Bill Dearden for a diving header – 1-0. A long ball from Currie into Dearden saw the latter tripped for a penalty. Alan Woodward converted via the underside of the crossbar to win the game 2-1.

Alan Warboys made his Sheffield United debut away at Liverpool, on 23 September. Liverpool won 5-0.

Goldthorpe-born Warboys had started his career at Doncaster, making his debut aged 17. After 40 appearances and 12 goals, he signed for Sheffield Wednesday. He was still only 18 when Jack Marshall took him to S6. In 1970 the Owls were relegated, and Warboys was sold to Cardiff City for £42,000, as a replacement for Liverpool-bound John Toshack. His Cardiff City debut was against his former employers, Wednesday. He thanked them for selling him by scoring two goals against them. He spent two seasons in Wales, before coming back to Sheffield for the red half.

An Alan Woodward penalty was just enough for the Blades to beat Manchester United 1-0 at Bramall Lane at the end of September, and Dearden scored the winner against Arsenal at the start of October to lift the Blades to seventh in the table.

Between the Manchester United and Arsenal games, the Blades drew 0-0 with Charlton Athletic in the third round of the League Cup. They drew the replay 2-2, Currie and Woodward scoring for the Blades. Bill Dearden scored the winner in the second replay to seal a fourth-round tie with the Gunners.

Blades fans planned to enjoy a sunny 14 October when United travelled to Upton Park to face a West Ham side unbeaten at home. Sheffield United had only lost once on the road, so were quietly confident facing a side that included Bobby Moore, Billy Bonds, Frank Lampard, Trevor Brooking and Brian Robson. Already depleted, United lost Bill Dearden to injury; McAlister, Goulding, Hemsley, Flynn, Colquhoun, Hockey, Woodward, Badger, Warboys, Currie and Holmes were in the Blades' starting XI.

Pre-match talk was of Frank Lampard versus Tony Currie, both looking to impress the watching England manager, Sir Alf Ramsey. Brooking scored with a half-volley on 16 minutes, after Currie had initially lost the ball and failed to win it back. Warboys missed a sitter, heading it over the bar, then Robson quickly added a second. Woodward went close from distance and then pulled a shot wide from 20 yards, but Robson made it 3-0 by half-time.

An own goal by Tommy Tyler while trying to clear a quick free kick from Woodward got one back in a better second half, but it was not enough for the win.

Against Everton, United had the ball in the net in the first minute but it was ruled out for offside. The referee had initially waved play-on but after he conferred with the linesman, changed his mind.

Despite a lively start to the second half, and Steve Goulding smashing a left-footed effort against the bar from 40 yards, Joe Royle set up Whittle for the only goal of the game.

At the Baseball Ground, against Derby County, United were a goal down at the break to a Colin Todd pile-driver. In the second half, United pushed five men into the box for a corner and Currie got on the end of it to score the equaliser. He celebrated by sticking two fingers up to the crowd. Derby added a winner later when McAlister saved a penalty, only to see the rebound scored.

Three days later, defender Ted Hemsley scored a consolation as United were knocked out of the League Cup by Arsenal. A goalless draw at Bramall Lane against Stoke City on 4 November at least gave the Blades a clean sheet, but three defeats in a row followed, away against Leeds United and Coventry City and then at home against Wolves, where Dearden was knocked unconscious while scoring with a diving header.

Between 7 October and 28 December, United won just once in 12 games and were plummeting towards the relegation zone. A rare 2-0 win over Leicester City, on 16 December, was followed by three further defeats to Tottenham, Liverpool and Newcastle United.

Midfielder Mick Speight returned to the first team in the defeat at St James' Park. Speight had first signed for the Blades in 1969, but his appearances had largely been restricted to the reserves, with the odd outing for the first team as a substitute or occasional cover. Hockey was dropped in December and replaced by Keith Eddy. Speight came in for a run of five games.

New Year's Day, 1973, saw the United Kingdom become a fully-fledged member of the European Economic Community. Ireland and Denmark also joined the EEC. The occasion was marked in Brussels by a Union flag being raised at the EEC headquarters. An optimistic Ted Heath hoped joining would bring prosperity to the country, saying, 'It's going to be gradual development, and obviously things won't happen overnight. But from the point of view of our everyday lives we will find there is a great cross-fertilisation of knowledge and information, not only in business but in every other sphere. And this will enable us to be more efficient and more competitive in gaining more markets not only in Europe but in the rest of the world.'

Five days later, at home to West Bromwich Albion, Bill Dearden scored twice, and Mackenzie got one to make it 3-0, and when Keith Eddy scored the winner against Watford a week later in the FA Cup third round, United fans perhaps thought the new year had brought some new cheer. However, by February, United were out of the cup after losing to Second Division Carlisle United.

Scottish striker Jim Bone was signed from Norwich City to partner Bill Dearden, and made his debut away at Leicester City in a 0-0 draw on 24 February.

Twenty-two-year-old Bone had played at Partick Thistle for four years before moving to the Canaries. He scored 50 goals in 107 games for Thistle, helping them clinch promotion back to the Scottish First Division. In his time at Norwich, he managed nine goals. One of those was Norwich City's first ever goal in the top flight, after he helped them to promotion the previous year.

It would be March before United won again, beating Crystal Palace 1-0, Dearden scoring the goal. A week later they lost again, at Everton – despite Bone scoring his first goal for the Blades.

On Monday, 23 April, Bobby Charlton made his final appearance at Old Trafford. Charlton, the nephew of Newcastle legend Jackie Milburn, had made his debut for the Red Devils in 1956, had survived the Munich air disaster aged just 20, and had gone on to play over 600 times. He played for England 106 times, scoring a record-breaking 49 goals. He was also Manchester United's record goalscorer for many years, until Wayne Rooney beat both his records.

In his final bow in front of more than 55,000 fans at Old Trafford, his side were beaten 1-2. Brian Kidd gave Manchester the lead, but Dearden equalised before Keith Eddy scored the winner to ruin Sir Bobby's farewell. Charlton's last game was away at Chelsea.

Striker Bill Dearden recalls, 'The atmosphere was unbelievable. I grew up near there, in Oldham, but we never had enough money to go to games when we were kids, so to actually play at Old Trafford in such a memorable game with a player like Bobby Charlton was brilliant. And to score a goal, blumming heck.'

Tony Currie was approached by Manchester United to replace Charlton, but as TC describes it, he signed his life away to the Blades instead.

A draw at Ipswich Town, and victory at home to Tottenham on the last day of the season saw United finish 14th in the table, with 40 points.

Liverpool won the title with 60 points, three points above runners-up Arsenal. Bill Dearden ended the season as United's top scorer with 20 goals, with Alan Woodward his nearest rival with half that amount.

Chapter 8

WITH PLANS for the new stand going ahead at considerable expense, money was still tight and there was little cash for transfers. A matchday programme cost 7p in 1973.

United had a decent but small squad and any injuries would mean the Blades would struggle for cover. John Harris did make one signing, raiding Watford once more, this time for Colin Franks. Franks had started his career as a midfielder but could also play in defence. He had made 112 appearances for the Hornets, including a memorable run in the 1969/70 FA Cup. When Watford were relegated to the Third Division, United paid £60,000 for his services.

On 7 August 1973, Yorkshire and Lancashire met in the last cricket match ever played at Bramall Lane, bringing an end to over 100 years of first-class cricket in Sheffield. The three-day 'war of the roses' finished in a draw.

United started their third season in Division One at home to Burnley on 25 August. It ended 0-2 to the visitors. Three days later at Molineux, United lost again by the same scoreline, leaving them bottom of the table. Chelsea, a couple of places above the Blades, but also without a win, were the next opponents. Dave Sexton's Chelsea included Ron 'Chopper' Harris, Alan Hudson, Peter Osgood, John Hollins and Peter Bonetti in goal. The game was televised, somewhat of a novelty in those days, with the brilliant Brian Moore commentating. Chelsea themselves were in the process of building a revolutionary three-tier stand. The Chelsea owners believed that their superstar players should play in a ground befitting of them. They initially planned to build an ambitious, 50,000 all-seater stadium. Many Chelsea fans believe the plans were too ambitious and that they were responsible for bringing about the downfall of the club, forcing the sale of its players, followed by relegation. The ground has been totally revamped since the 1990s, but the magnificent three-tier stand remains.

Clive Thomas, the colourful and often controversial referee disallowed a Chelsea goal from a John Hollins free kick, which found an unmarked Thomas Hutchinson. There was no flag from the linesman, but Clive Thomas judged that Hutchinson had pushed a defender.

Thomas later gave a controversial penalty for handball against Badger, when he appeared to be protecting his face. Badger, on his 30th birthday, was shown the yellow card for dissent following his protests. Hollins smashed the ball into the roof of the net from the spot, giving McAlister no chance.

Chelsea continued to press United, having a string of corners before Tony Currie won the ball on the edge of the Chelsea area, then let fly, hitting the ball into the top corner with his right foot just before half-time. As the game went on, Currie was playing exceptionally well, spraying long passes around and setting up several chances that United wasted. Bone sent Woodward clear with 15 minutes remaining and Bonetti fumbled the shot which squirmed under him to make it 1-2 United, sealing Chelsea's third defeat in three games.

With United full of confidence, the Blades welcomed Arsenal to Bramall Lane three days later, on the Tuesday night. The Blades raced into an early lead and many fans missed the opening goal from Bill Dearden. Some missed the second from Alan Woodward and some arrived to find their team leading 3-0.

It was four by half-time.

The fans who missed the early goals were given something to cheer later, when Currie copied what Alan Ball had done a couple of seasons before. Ball had sat on the ball in the centre circle, but with United cruising at 4-0, Currie decided to sit down on the ball inside his own penalty area.

In 2020, Brazilian superstar Neymar received a booking for attempting a rainbow flick during PSG's 5-0 thrashing of Montpellier, as it was judged by the referee Jerome Brisard as unsporting. I dread to think what referees today would make of TC squatting down on the ball in his own 18-yard box. The game ended 5-0 to the Blades and Currie scored two of them to round off his show.

He was called up to Alf Ramsey's England squad and on 26 September – the same day that Concorde made its first nonstop crossing of the Atlantic – England beat Austria 7-0. Currie made two of the goals and scored his first for his country, a lovely volley from the edge of the box, after taking the ball down on his chest.

Keith Eddy was injured in the 1-0 win at home to Norwich City and would miss the next 14 games. Franks came in for him against Southampton at the Dell; United lost 3-0.

At home to Leicester City, in October, Currie beat two men before being tripped and winning a penalty – converted by Alan Woodward against Currie's England team-mate, Peter Shilton.

Woodward scored again two days later in the League Cup second round at West Bromwich Albion, this time getting the winner.

Speight made his first start of the season away at Stoke City. Woodward was on target for the third time in three games, Scullion also scoring in the 1-2 win.

Away at Manchester City, a game which ended in a 2-1 defeat, goalkeeper Tom McAlister was seriously injured. A weakened Sheffield United went to Anfield the following week and lost 1-0, with John Connaughton making a rare appearance in goal.

In November, United's poor form continued, the Blades winning just once. Coventry City, United's opponents on 24 November, had not scored a goal in over 600 minutes of football before they took the lead. Woodward smashed an equaliser from outside the area, with a blistering free kick. Free kicks were well into double figures in what could be described as a feisty game (remembering tackles were tackles and seldom punished in those days).

Currie also had the ball in the net, from yet another free kick, but it was disallowed. Two goals in the last quarter of an hour saw Coventry win 3-1.

With United 13th in the league and 19 points behind leaders Leeds United, the board decided action was needed and changes had to be made. Harris, who had been at the club for 14 years, resigned as manager for the second time, this time to become the senior executive of the club, so that they could employ a new 'tracksuit' manager.

On 9 December, they opted for Ken Furphy.

Furphy had played in the lower leagues for Darlington before being named player-manager at Watford, where he won promotion in 1969. There, he worked with Tony Currie, Stuart Scullion and Keith Eddy.

In 1971, new Blackburn Rovers chairman, William Bancroft, offered the young manager the challenge of reviving the club's fortunes, following Rovers' relegation to the Third Division for the first time in their history. He steered them to a tenth-place finish in his first season, before guiding them to a 19-match unbeaten run, which resulted in them achieving third place in 1972/73.

He was still only in his early 40s when he joined United, and wearing his tracksuit, he struck a very different picture on the touchline to John Harris. Furphy was known to favour forging strong links to the communities and the club thought this was what was needed, with the investment in the ground taking shape.

In 1969, Furphy had become the first ever manager to allow a pre-match team-talk to be televised. Before Watford's FA Cup fourth-round clash with Manchester United, Furphy allowed BBC's *Grandstand* programme to eavesdrop on his instructions. United fans didn't exactly welcome the new manager initially, perhaps fearing change after having 'Gentleman John' at the helm for so long. Furphy's appointment felt like a step into the unknown.

The day after Furphy was unveiled as Blades boss, United drew 0-0 with Queens Park Rangers at Loftus Road. The following week, Eddie Colquhoun scored in a 1-1 draw with Everton.

Three days before Christmas, United enjoyed their first victory under Ken Furphy, a 4-2 win at Bramall Lane against

Southampton, by which time United were 14th in the table. Alan Woodward scored a hat-trick and the new manager's old protege, Tony Currie, scored the other.

On Boxing Day, United made it back-to-back wins for the first time since September, beating Manchester United 1-2 at Old Trafford, Currie and Woodward again winning the plaudits and scoring the goals.

United's winning streak was short-lived though, and they lost the next two league games and lost in the FA Cup third round, away at Ipswich Town. They won just one of their next ten games, the exception coming at Burnley.

Despite the club's financial predicament, Furphy was allowed to sign goalkeeper Jim Brown from Chesterfield. Brown had made his debut in Scotland with Albion Rovers at the age of 16. He made 94 appearances for the men from Coatbridge before being spotted by Chesterfield in a friendly against them. He quickly established himself as a first-team regular at Saltergate, making 47 appearances, before moving to Bramall Lane on transfer deadline day for £70,000.

Tony Field, who Furphy had signed for Blackburn, was bought for £76,666 as well as Terry Garbett for £30,000.

Two self-proclaimed British government spies escaped from jail in Ireland on 11 March. Kenneth and Keith Littlejohn were locked up for armed robbery, after stealing £67,000. During their trial, the brothers claimed they were working for the government, against the IRA. The government denied their claims and when the pair exhausted all their avenues of appeal, they scaled a 25-foot wall with home-made ropes, while other inmates distracted guards. The younger of the two was injured during the escape and was quickly recaptured. Big brother Kenneth, who had been on hunger strike for a month, evaded capture for over a year and a half. They were released in 1981, on condition that they left Ireland. They did, and six years later, Kenneth was returned to prison after an armed robbery in Chesterfield.

Brown and Field both made their United debuts against Manchester City on 16 March. The game was decided by a single goal from Geoff Salmons. Tony Field scored his first goal for United a week later in a 1-0 win over West Ham United. The Blades then beat Liverpool by a single goal, taking them to tenth, but then lost to Derby County and Leeds United.

Alan Woodward scored the winner in the last game of the season, away at Ipswich Town.

United finished a respectable 13th in the league, but early exits from both of the cups, and the ongoing development of the new South Stand, meant selling more players was inevitable.

Geoff Salmons was sold to Stoke City for a fee of £170,000 to ease the burden. Stuart Scullion was sold back to Watford, and Staniforth and Bone were also shipped out for considerably less significant sums.

Alan Woodward was voted player of the year and was top scorer with 12 goals.

Leeds United won the 1973/74 Division One title but their long-serving manager Don Revie would soon depart to take over the role of England manager. His replacement at Elland Road was Brian Clough.

Clough's appointment raised a few eyebrows, as Clough had previously been critical of both Revie and his team –

accusing them of being dirty and calling them cheats. Clough approached the job in his usual forthright way, upsetting many of the senior players on his arrival by telling them to throw their league title winners' medals in the bin. His short time in charge is well documented, both in print and in the semi-factual adaptation, *The Damned United*.

Southampton and Norwich City were relegated, along with Manchester United, who finished the season in 21st place.

Bill Shankly's Liverpool won the FA Cup Final but in July, their sombre chairman John Smith announced, 'It is with great regret that I as chairman of Liverpool Football Club, have to inform you that Mr Shankly has intimated that he wishes to retire from active participation in league football. And the board has with extreme reluctance accepted his decision. I would like to at this stage place on record the board's great appreciation of Mr Shankly's magnificent achievements over the period of his managership.'

Shankly, 60, who had been at the club for 15 years, said, 'The pressures have built up so much during my 40 years in the game, that I felt it was time to have a rest.'

During his time at Anfield, Shankly won promotion to the First Division, won the league title three times, the FA Cup and the UEFA Cup. Much of the success that Liverpool would achieve in the late 70s and early 80s under Bob Paisley and Joe Fagan was built on foundations laid by Shankly. In November 1974 he received the OBE and remained in the city until his death in 1981.

Chapter 9

PRE-SEASON FOR Ken Furphy's Blades began in Poland. Furphy liked to bring players with him when he moved clubs, and midfielder David Bradford was bought from Blackburn Rovers for £10,000.

Bradford made his debut in the opening game of the trip to central Europe, a goalless draw against second division Lechia FC. He kept his place for the 3-1 defeat to Pogon, three days later. United drew the next game 2-2 and won the last game of the tour 1-0.

On returning to England, United took part in the Texaco Cup. Initially including teams from England, Scotland, Ireland and Northern Ireland, the cup had first been staged in 1970/71, when Wolves beat Hearts 3-2 in the final. In its third season, the Irish didn't take part and the £100,000 prize was contested between six English teams and six Scottish. United took part that season but Ipswich Town won the cup, beating their fierce rivals Norwich City in the final.

For the 1974/75 tournament the organisers changed the format, with 16 teams from England playing in the group phase, before being joined by Scottish clubs in the knockout stages. This would be the final year the tournament was contested.

United began against Oldham Athletic and were thrashed 4-0. Two days later, United bounced back and beat Manchester City 4-2, with two goals from Tony Currie and one each for Bill Dearden and Alan Woodward. Woodward scored again in the 1-1 draw with Blackpool but United finished bottom of Group C and were eliminated. The two-legged final was won by Newcastle United, beating Southampton 3-1.

The new season started at home to Queens Park Rangers. Just over 16,000 were at the Lane to see Steve Cammack give United a first-half lead, but Rangers equalised and the game ended 1-1.

Two away games followed, first at St James' Park, where the Blades drew 2-2 with Newcastle, and then at the Baseball Ground, where United were beaten 2-0 by Derby County.

United's first victory of the season came on 27 August, when Newcastle United were beaten 2-1 at the Lane by goals from Tony Field and Cammack, a striker who was another of the Sheffield-born players at Bramall Lane. He signed for United in 1971 as a 17-year-old, but never managed to hold down a regular place in the side.

Cammack came in as cover for Bill Dearden against Newcastle, but his goal wasn't enough to keep his place and Dearden returned for the next game, a 3-1 win over Ipswich Town. Mick Mills scored an own goal after great work in the box from Woodward, jinking left and right before shooting against the post – the rebound hitting the unfortunate Mills and bouncing over the line. Tony Field added another with a deflected shot, but needed no help for his second, beating three men and driving into the box before chipping the advancing keeper. A superb solo effort for his third goal in two games.

Another win followed, this time away at West Ham United. Alan Woodward scored one and Bill Dearden justified his return to the side with a goal. Keith Eddy then got the winner at home to Middlesbrough in United's fourth consecutive win in the league, lifting them to fourth in the table.

Early-season dreams of challenging for a place in Europe or even winning the title, were quickly dashed by a trouncing away at Leeds United. By the time United visited Elland Road, Brian Clough had already departed and had been replaced by former Blackpool favourite, Jimmy Armfield. Clough lasted just 44 days in the Leeds hotseat. During that time, Leeds won just once in their opening six games and had gained just four points when the board decided they had made a mistake and sacked Clough. Unfortunately for United, they faced a rejuvenated Leeds as they were recovering from Clough's reign, and Leeds ran out comfortable 5-1 winners. Bill Dearden, who had hit the post early on in the game, got the consolation for the Blades.

Alan Woodward scored two in two games; the opener in the 1-1 draw with Wolves, and the winner at home to Liverpool, when he beat the offside trap brilliantly from a Tony Currie through-ball before slotting under the goalie.

United were beaten 3-2 at Roker Park, then new signing David Bradford scored his first goal for the club in a 2-0 win at home to Luton Town in the League Cup.

A 2-2 draw with Everton was covered by Yorkshire TV. A low cross from Woodward, converted by Dearden in the six-yard box, gave United an early lead. Woodward's superb half-volley from outside the box doubled United's lead, before they let Everton come back into the game, eventually drawing level. The draw was followed by two defeats in October, first at home to Derby, then a 3-0 loss at Filbert Street.

> On 22 October, a bomb exploded inside Brooks Club in London. Conservative leader Ted Heath was dining nearby but wasn't thought to be the target. Although several of the waiters were injured in the blast, all the diners had already left, and there were no fatalities. The Provisional IRA were blamed for the attack, which was thought to be part of a spate of similar bombings in the capital that year. 1974 was one of the IRA's most prolific bombing sprees. In June, a bomb had exploded at the Houses of Parliament, injuring 11 people. At the start of the year, a coach ferrying soldiers was blown up on the M60, killing 12 people, including at least two children. Later that year, Heath was targeted, when a device exploded outside his home. Just days after the Brooks Club attack, the wife of sports minister, Denis Howell, survived an attack. Her Ford Cortina was blown up as she reversed out of the family's drive. She and her son, who was also in the car, miraculously escaped, despite the windows of the house being shattered by the explosion.

Following the back-to-back defeats in the Midlands, United won four on the bounce. Dearden, Woodward and Eddy scored in the 3-2 win over Birmingham City at Bramall Lane. United beat Rotherham United on penalties in the County Cup and beat Carlisle United and Luton Town to retain fourth place.

Alan Woodward and Keith Eddy both scored in a 2-2 draw with Norwich City in the fourth round of the League Cup, but the Canaries went on to win the replay 2-1. Following their exit from the cup, United lost three games in a row. Spurs beat them 0-1 at the Lane, Manchester United won 3-2, and the Blades then went down 1-0 at Loftus Road. The defeat to QPR saw United drop to mid-table, before Bill Dearden scored the winner at home against Coventry City the week before Christmas.

> On Christmas Eve, former Labour minister John Stonehouse was found alive in Australia after attempting to fake his own death. Stonehouse was thought to have drowned when he disappeared on a business trip to Florida and a pile of his clothes was left on the sand at Miami beach. It was suspected that the politician planned to start a new life with his secretary but he ended up being jailed for seven years. His lover was jailed for two years.

United were beaten 1-0 by Middlesbrough at Ayresome Park on Boxing Day, and two days later they drew 1-1 with Arsenal. The Gunners took the lead, but Field latched on to the end of a Woodward ball to level the score. United had now won just once in nine games.

Just over 20,000 were back inside Bramall Lane on 4 January 1975 for the FA Cup third round tie against Bristol City. The majority of the fans went home happy after United won 2-0.

A third home game in a row saw United draw 1-1 with eighth-placed Manchester City. United then travelled to White Hart Lane to face a struggling Tottenham Hotspur side. Spurs had beaten Newcastle the previous week, 2-5, but had gone four without a win prior to that.

John Duncan gave Spurs the lead, but Currie levelled after a goalmouth scramble. Eddy found himself furthest forward to get on the end of a Field cross to make it 1-2, before Woodward beat the advancing Pat Jennings from well outside the penalty box to make it 1-3. The win lifted United to 11th in the First Division.

United went down 4-1 at Villa Park in the fourth round of the FA Cup, before drawing at home to Luton Town in the league. The Blades beat Carlisle United 1-0 and then beat Chelsea at Bramall Lane – goals from Woodward and Badger sealing the win. They lost away at Burnley 2-1 then beat Ipswich Town by a single goal. Woodward was on target in both games. Eddie Colquhoun scored a rare goal at home to Wolves, which was enough to take both points.

> On 4 March, silent film actor Charlie Chaplin was knighted. He and his fourth wife Oona, along with two of their nine children, attended Buckingham Palace to receive the honour. This recognition for 86-year-old Chaplin had been delayed several times, due to him courting controversy. As well as being suspected of communism, two of his wives were only 16 when he married them.

A goalless draw at Anfield saw United continue to climb the table. When they faced West Ham United on 22 March, Bobby Gould gave the Hammers the lead but Tony Currie equalised minutes later, tapping into the net from close range. It was Currie who had started the move, lofting a high ball into the area, brilliantly controlled by Woodward, who played it in low to find Currie, who had continued his run and was standing on the goal line. West Ham regained the lead when a speculative overhead kick, which should have been caught easily by Brown, was inexplicably fumbled into the United goal. Woodward equalised for the Blades, this time coming in from the left. Cammack's long ball was taken down effortlessly by Woodward and slotted coolly into the net for 2-2.

The best goal was yet to come. After a scrappy bit of head tennis, Tony Currie intercepted in his own half. A one-two with Woodward found Currie with space to run into and options to either side of him. Currie continued to carry the ball, jinking one way then the other, throwing in a step-over, before placing a pass with his left foot into the corner of the net. Keeper Mervyn Day was helpless.

'What about that!' exclaimed John Moston. 'A quality goal by a quality player.'

The Blades failed to win their next two games, losing 1-0 at Highbury and drawing 1-1 with Leeds United. Keith Eddy and Tony Field scored the goals that beat high-flying Stoke City 2-0 at Bramall Lane. That result put United just two points behind the Potters.

On 19 April 1975, United faced Everton, who had themselves been chasing a place in Europe earlier in the season, but recent results had been inconsistent. The Toffees had beaten Newcastle United in their previous game but had lost to Luton Town and, surprisingly, at bottom-of-the-league Carlisle before that, so the game was something of a must-win for both sides.

The home side drew first blood with a left-footer from Welsh international David Smallman. Currie and Woodward stood over a free kick, but Currie played it square to Badger who rattled the woodwork from 25 yards. Everton, though, doubled their lead from the penalty spot with just over half an hour played. In the second half, a terrific corner from Alan Woodward found the head of Keith Eddy to make it 2-1.

Badger, getting forward and overlapping down the right, put in a cross that the Everton keeper couldn't deal with, and Bill Dearden was on hand for 2-2. With just over five minutes left a long ball from Badger found Tony Field, who crossed first time for Tony Currie to volley in the winner.

Derby County, Liverpool, Ipswich Town, Everton, Stoke, Middlesbrough and United were now all battling for the lucrative four European places. United had a game in hand on the other teams. Everton only had one game left, against Chelsea, while Stoke City had a trip to Burnley in their final game.

United's game in hand was at home to struggling Leicester City. David Bradford scored the first goal after good play from Mick Speight. A Tony Currie corner was headed home by John Flynn to make it 2-0, before Currie scored a long-range effort to put United three up at the break. In the second half, United continued to dominate and Field was brought down in front of a packed Kop to win a penalty. Up stepped Keith Eddy to convert the kick and make the score Sheffield United 4, Leicester City 0. 'And it's one more stride towards Europe,' declared the commentator on TV.

The win meant that if United won their final game, away at Birmingham, and Stoke lost to Burnley, then United had a chance of securing fourth place. A draw would put them level with Stoke but they had the far superior goal difference.

Birmingham had beaten Newcastle in their last game, but had lost four on the bounce prior to that, conceding nine goals.

Striker Bill Dearden says, 'We all believed we could do it. You have to. You go out there at three o'clock, thinking "we are going to win two points today". We believed we could beat anyone. No one was better than us. The United side that was promoted to the Premier League in 2019 reminded me of us. We'd take anyone on.'

Midfielder Micky Speight echoed the thought, 'Yes, we should have been there. We had a very good side and played great attacking football.'

United reportedly took 6,000 fans to St Andrew's, eagerly hoping for a flurry of goals. The game ended 0-0 and United finished sixth, level on points with Stoke City – who picked up a point on that final Saturday – one behind Everton and just four points behind champions Derby County. It was United's best finish since 1962. Had it not been for the run of poor results through November and early December, who knows how close United might have got to competing with the very best teams in Europe?

Division One table 1974/75

	Played	*W*	*D*	*L*	*Points*
1 Derby County	42	21	11	10	53
2 Liverpool	42	20	11	11	51
3 Ipswich Town	42	23	5	14	51
4 Everton	42	16	18	8	50
5 Stoke City	42	17	15	10	49
6 Sheffield United	42	18	13	11	49

Chapter 10

EARLY IN the summer, United signed Chris Guthrie from Third Division Southend United for around £90,000, despite the ever-growing money worries caused by the building of the new South Stand.

Guthrie had started at Newcastle United, where he was part of the youth team that won the prestigious International Youth Cup in Rotterdam, and had played at schoolboy level for England before joining Southend in 1972. He had scored 35 goals in just over 100 games for them. His older brother Ron, a defender, had also been a Newcastle player before joining their closest rivals Sunderland and featuring in their FA Cup victory in 1973.

After playing friendlies abroad, United took part in the first Anglo-Scottish Cup during pre-season. The competition was a reincarnation of the Texaco Cup and featured a total of 16 teams, eight each from either side of the border. The Scottish teams competed against each other, as did the English teams, then the top four from each nation crossed the border to play each other in the quarter-finals. The organisers were keen to protect the integrity of the cup and encouraged teams to field their strongest XI. To emphasise this point, in the following season Newcastle were thrown out of the tournament for fielding a weakened side.

In the inaugural tournament the Blades complied. Len Badger, Keith Eddy and Alan Woodward all scored in a 3-1 win over Blackburn, and Speight scored in the 1-1 draw with Blackpool. Woodward scored United's only goal, from a free kick, in a 3-1 loss to Manchester City and United failed to make the quarter-final stage. New man Guthrie started in the Anglo-Scottish games, replacing Bill Dearden.

United's opening two league fixtures were both at Bramall Lane, complete with the newly finished new South Stand. Currie missed them both through suspension, Tony Garbutt taking his place. Keith Eddy scored a penalty in both games, first in a 1-1 draw with reigning league champions Derby County, then in a 1-3 defeat against Arsenal, in which John Flynn dislocated his shoulder, an injury which would keep him out for a month.

The cricket pitch at Headingley was vandalised by protesters on 19 August. The campaigners called for George Davis – a London taxi driver – to be freed from prison after being convicted of robbing the London Electricity Board office. As well as digging holes in the pitch, they daubed 'George Davis is innocent' and 'Justice for George Davis' on the walls. Four men appeared in court for the vandalism, but their actions resulted in an inquiry into Davis's arrest which led to him being released after the inquiry raised serious questions about his conviction. The Who singer Roger Daltrey appeared on stage wearing a T-shirt supporting Davis and Sham 69's

> debut album, *Tell us the Truth*, has a track titled 'George Davis is Innocent'. Two years later he was sentenced to 15 years for his part in a robbery at the Bank of Cyprus, which he pleaded guilty to. Following his release in 1984, he was once again jailed, in 1987, for attempting to steal mail bags.

On 23 August 1975, Sheffield United were the first visitors to Old Trafford, following Manchester United's return to the top flight under manager Tommy Docherty. Manchester had spent just one season in the Second Division. It was the first time they'd played in the second tier since 1938. Despite relegation, the average attendance at Old Trafford during their triumphant cameo was 47,781, higher than any First Division side's. Their 2-0 defeat at Villa Park, in February, had been their last. Docherty's young team had won their opening two games of the new season, away from home, raising expectations, and they were already being tipped by some as would-be champions. The Blades had picked up one point thus far, in the home draw with Derby County.

Tony Currie returned to the side after completing his suspension and was due to play for England against Switzerland the following week. A crowd of 55,949 packed inside Old Trafford and the noise was deafening as the home fans sang 'Glory, Glory Man United'.

When Stuart Pearson made it 1-0 for the champions-elect in the tenth minute, the chant changed to 'CHAMPIONS! CHAMPIONS!' After 38 minutes, they added a second goal, after Woodward uncharacteristically gave the ball away several times, McIlroy eventually taking advantage. Five minutes before half-time, keeper Jim Brown dropped a cross and Pearson tapped home his second goal of the game from one yard.

Garbutt came on for Len Badger at half-time, with the Blades trailing 3-0. Ten minutes after the restart, Guthrie pulled one back when he was left unmarked in the box, raising the faint possibility of mounting a comeback. However, just after the hour, Daley added number four, and Sammy McIlroy made it 5-1 ten minutes from the end.

Three days later, on the Tuesday night, at Goodison Park, there was little improvement. Goulding came in for Badger, but United slipped to another defeat, this time losing 3-0. The Blades had conceded eight goals in three days and scored just once.

The following Saturday, Leeds United were the visitors at the new and improved, even more beautiful downtown Bramall Lane. Jimmy Armfield's side had lost only one of their opening four games but came to the Lane on the back of a 3-0 defeat to Liverpool. Despite the odds not looking good for the Blades, and a dreadful run of results, over 30,000 fans paid to watch the Yorkshire derby.

Mackenzie scored his first goal of the season for Leeds with a diving header in the first half and Allan Clarke scored with a bobbling shot from outside the area to make it 2-0 in the second period. It was United's fifth game without a win and next up were Liverpool.

Len Badger was recalled for the trip to Anfield after coming off the bench against Leeds. Ted Hemsley also returned for the Blades. A battling United performance kept Liverpool out for almost 80 minutes, before Ray Kennedy scored the only goal of the game to leave United bottom of the league and still without a win in six attempts.

Third Division Halifax Town gave the United fans a rare cheer on 10 September in the second round of the League Cup. With Furphy desperate for a win, he fielded an unchanged team, and was rewarded with a Chris Guthrie hat-trick. An own goal from Halifax's Phelan made it 2-4 on the night.

Back to the dreadful reality of the disastrous league campaign, and United's next game was at home to Coventry City. Coventry had already beaten Manchester City and Everton and got a good point against Manchester United. They sat ninth in the table and 20,153 fans turned up at Bramall Lane to see the home side lose, yet again.

On 20 September, still without a win in the league and with just one point from their opening seven games, the Blades travelled to Upton Park. Cliff Calvert replaced Ted Hemsley, and Len Badger was absent again as United were beaten 2-0 to heap more gloom on the fans and more pressure on Furphy.

Burnley had drawn three of their first four fixtures at the start of the season but had beaten Middlesbrough and drawn 4-4 with Norwich City and found themselves in 17th position, with seven points from eight games, when they visited rock-bottom Blades on Tuesday, 23 September. Level at half-time thanks to a Guthrie goal, fans in the new South Stand finally saw their first home win when Tony Field scored the winner in the second half.

In defiance of the dismal form and the ominous position in the league, the fans remained remarkably positive, and over 21,000 were there to witness and celebrate United's first league win in 900 minutes of First Division football. They hadn't tasted success since 26 April – more than 150 days earlier.

Unfortunately, United lost their next two games without finding the net: 0-1 at home to Norwich City and 2-0 away at Birmingham City on 4 October.

On 1 October, world champion Muhammad Ali retained his title in a fight dubbed 'The Thrilla in Manila'. An estimated global audience of one billion people watched Ali beat arch-rival Joe Frazier in their third fight, one of the most brutal in history. After a blistering attack in the 13th round, Ali sent Frazier's gumshield flying with a flurry of punches. Frazier was stopped at the end of the 14th round when his trainer Eddie Futch threw in the towel. Ali said afterwards that the fight was the closest thing to dying. While the bout is often described as the greatest ever, Frazier was not at his peak. He was suffering from arthritis in his shoulder, and according to his biography, published many years later, he was also partially blind. A dodgy speed ball, used during his training regime, had caused splinters in his eye. With the other one badly swollen by the punishment Ali administered, Frazier was probably almost sightless when Futch intervened.

Smokin' Joe wasn't finished though. He fought George Foreman in 1976. The two had met previously in '73, when Frazier lost his title and his undefeated record. He had gone 29 bouts without losing prior to the first meeting. He lost again in the second match, when a huge punch from Foreman lifted Frazier off his feet.

Ali's best years were also well behind him. He continued to box, beating a string of opponents, including Brit Richard Dunn and Ken Norton. In 1978 he fought the inexperienced Leon Spinks. Spinks had fought in just seven pro bouts, and Ali barely trained for the fight. He was not in good shape at all and lost the bout in a split decision. In September the same year, the two met again and Ali became the first heavyweight to win the title three times.

United's defeat at Birmingham proved to be the final straw for Ken Furphy, and on 6 October, the 44-year-old was sacked. United were rooted firmly to the foot of the table, already adrift with just four points – three behind Wolves, who were second from bottom. United had won just once since the start of the season. Some fans believed the board had acted too soon, and some players thought Furphy should have been given longer, particularly considering his achievements the previous season. Good managers don't become bad ones overnight.

Furphy managed to keep his reputation somewhat intact; it was largely believed that he had done a good job under difficult circumstances. He had guided the Blades to their best finish in over a decade and got them playing some of the most exciting football in the country. You might also argue that he had taken some inadequate players from his former surroundings of the Third Division, that simply weren't good enough for the top level, and planted them unsuccessfully in the First Division; but it seems he was forgiven that and was soon back in work.

After leaving the Steel City, he headed across the pond to New York. He managed New York Cosmos, who most famous player at the time was none other than the greatest ever footballer (no, not Tony Currie): Pele. Furphy would later continue the trend of re-signing his old players and raided United more than once. After minimal success at Cosmos he headed to Miami, Detroit and Washington, where he coached George Best, Bobby Moore and Johan Cruyff. There are not many managers or coaches that can boast having had those superstars in their teams. Most mortals would settle for having seen them play, let alone coached them.

His five years in America effectively ended his involvement in the game, and he never managed again after 1981, although he did spend a week as technical director of Exeter City in 2001.

He passed away in 2015, aged 83, after suffering from dementia. Although he managed some of the greatest names the game has ever seen, he is mostly fondly remembered for his time at Watford, winning promotion to the Second Division for the first time in their history.

Chapter 11

UNITED TURNED to Jimmy Sirrel. When the Sheffield United board appointed him, the team had won just once in 13 games.

Scotsman Sirrel had started his playing career as a forward at Celtic. From there he had moved to Bradford Park Avenue (an English Football League club until 1970), and then to Brighton and Aldershot and finally Brentford, where he was appointed manager in 1967.

He left Brentford two years later for Notts County. On his arrival at Meadow Lane, he is reported to have said confidently, 'Ask any kid what he knows about Notts County, and he'll tell you they're the oldest club in the world; by the time I'm finished he'll know a lot more.'

County had finished in the bottom half of the lowest league for the past three years when Sirrel left Brentford for them. True to his word, he took them from the old Fourth Division, where he found them, to the splendour of the First Division. He was not a glamorous man but filled his players with confidence and passion. He liked a solid defence but enjoyed fluid and lively attacking football. He once said that his goalkeeper was the most important member of his team because 'you start with a point and if he doesn't let a goal in, you keep that'.

After getting Notts County to the First Division, he managed to keep them there for three years. He achieved this remarkable success on a shoestring budget, so he had all the credentials required to fill the vacant manager's position at Bramall Lane. United were skint.

Sirrel was a serious manager, who believed that practice made perfect. To enforce the point, training usually consisted almost entirely of making the players take part in practice matches. Some of the players were not keen on the new man's methods.

Michael Speight says, 'Different managers have different ways of playing the game and you just had to adjust. But I think you have to choose a manager that has the same philosophy as the club. It's important to develop players and to carry on the club's traditional way of playing.'

United were in free-fall, at the bottom of the league, with a small, ageing squad, and no money to buy new players. Sirrel's first game in charge of the Blades was just a couple of days after his arrival, away at Wolverhampton Wanderers, on 11 October. At the start of play, Wolves were just a place above United in the table. Like United, they had only won once, but had lost fewer games and had managed to accumulate seven points compared to United's four. Both teams had scored four goals at home, but United had conceded more.

Away from home, United had lost five out of five, scored once and conceded 13. Wolves had also failed to win away from home and had also conceded 13 goals, but they had scored three times. It could barely be closer on paper, so United fans could have been forgiven for being optimistic before kick-off, under their new manager, hoping for a bounce. The game finished Wolverhampton Wanderers 5 Sheffield United 1.

The Blades' horrific form continued and they failed to find the net in their next two fixtures; a 0-2 home defeat to Stoke City and a 1-0 loss at Queens Park Rangers.

On 1 November, with Sirrel still looking for his first point as boss, United hosted Manchester City at Bramall Lane. Tommy Booth opened the scoring for City early on. Denis Tueart almost added a second, after a wayward pass from Woodward put City on the attack, but United keeper Tom McAlister saved brilliantly.

Peter Barnes added a second from an impossible angle, when sloppy defending from the Blades allowed him to keep the ball in play when it looked like going behind, from a deflected shot.

Within a minute of Barnes's goal though, Woodward lofted a ball high into the City box, which Guthrie managed to get his head to, and somehow succeeded in forcing the ball over the line, to make it 1-2.

Guthrie's goal was United's seventh of the season. A dubious-looking penalty threw United a lifeline. Seven minutes into the second half, a ball into the box from Currie was punched away by the keeper but to everyone's confusion, the referee pointed to the spot. Keith Eddy sent the City keeper the wrong way to make it 2-2.

Filled with belief and optimism after drawing with a decent Manchester City side, who had been in tenth place, United went to Villa Park the following week. Ron Saunders's Villa were having a mixed season and sat in 15th place. United conceded five for the third time that season, ending up on the wrong end of another 5-1 thrashing. Guthrie scored United's solitary goal.

Sirrel made his first move in the transfer market, signing former Scottish international Jimmy Johnstone on a free transfer and persuaded the board to pay £60,000 for Paul Garner from Huddersfield Town.

Johnstone had enjoyed a fabulous career at Celtic under the great Jock Stein, winning nine Scottish championships. 'Jinky' – as he was known to the Bhoys fans – had spent 13 seasons with the Scottish giants since making his debut in 1963. During that time, he played more than 300 games and scored over 80 goals. In his second season, he helped Celtic to a 5-0 win in the European Cup Winners' Cup, and was part of the Lisbon Lions, as Celtic became the first British team to win the European Cup, in 1967. He was nominated for the Ballon d'Or the same year. Despite his brilliance, he and Stein clashed many times, not least on one legendary evening in Germany, when the tiny Scot decided to take a boat out while inebriated and had to be rescued.

When his Celtic career finished, he headed to America, playing ten games for San Jose Earthquakes before arriving at Bramall Lane. By the time he turned up in Sheffield he was only a shadow of the player he had once been. His drinking was renowned, and now in his 30s, his best days were long behind him. He later admitted that after leaving Celtic his heart was no longer in playing football, but his arrival would still be met with some excitement.

Left-back Paul Garner had spent his career at Huddersfield Town, seeing them relegated from the top flight in his first season, and to the Fourth Division in his last season there.

The Bramall Lane faithful remained remarkably faithful and despite their team's evident decline, poor performances, regular thrashings, and almost certain relegation (already), over 20,000 were at the ground for the visit of Leicester City on 15 November. Garner made his United debut in place of veteran Ted Hemsley, but they lost 1-2, Alan Woodward scoring for the Blades.

Hemsley had played all but three games in the promotion season of 1970/71 and had been almost ever-present since. Now, under Sirrel, he found himself sidelined.

United were now ten points adrift of Burnley, who were second from bottom. They had conceded 39 goals in 15 games, and just scraped into double figures in the plus column.

Seventh-placed Stoke City were United's next opponents. Garner kept his place in the team and his new team-mate, Jimmy Johnstone, made his debut. It was a familiar name that stole the headlines though. Ex-United favourite Geoff Salmons – born in nearby Mexborough, and who played 180 games for the Blades – came back to haunt his former employers, scoring twice for Stoke, as United lost 2-1.

United gained a valuable point at Portman Road the following week, drawing 1-1 with Ipswich Town, narrowing the gap slightly on Burnley, who lost to Spurs. However, on 6 December, Burnley earned a point at home to Liverpool and the following week, on 13 December, they beat West Ham United 2-0.

United's calamitous season continued to worsen, as they lost 1-2 at home to Spurs on 6 December and were thrashed 1-4 at home to Manchester United on 13 December, to widen the gap again. Eddie Colquhoun's mistake led to the first Manchester goal inside two minutes for Stuart Pearson. Jim

Brown in the Blades' goal tried valiantly to keep out Gordon Hill, but after saving his first effort, could only watch as he rifled in the rebound from a tight angle to make it 2-0 at half-time. In the second half, Alan Woodward was tripped in the box to give United a penalty. Keith Eddy smashed the spot kick against the bar with the keeper beaten, but Bill Dearden rattled in the rebound on the volley.

Brown thwarted Steve Coppell from point-blank range as the home side showed resilience, despite being outclassed, but just moments later Pearson scored Manchester United's third. Lou Macari added the fourth after some shambolic defending from a corner.

The Blades were now 11 points behind Burnley, and a win for Birmingham City meant they were 12 points from safety, halfway through December.

Len Badger was cut from the team following the defeat at Old Trafford. He told author Nick Johnson, for his book *Match of My Life,* that the new manager liked big, strong types who could whack it and get up and down the pitch. He said Sirrel told him, 'Son, you're not big enough to play at the back.' Badger replied, 'Well Jim, I'm 31, I don't think I'm going to grow any more.' Sirrel's message was clear – find yourself another club. Badger had 18 months left on his contract but left the club right away. He admitted later that he regretted the decision. Len Badger loved Sheffield United, the club he had been at for 16 years, and he didn't really want to play at any other. His testimonial was later attended by 23,000 fans, such was his popularity at the Lane.

When he left United, he was signed up by his next-door neighbour at the time, former Blades favourite, Joe Shaw, who was now manager at Chesterfield. There, he played in 46 games before breaking a leg. After recovering, he played a few reserve games before making his first-team comeback against Tranmere at Saltergate. When he went in for a challenge, the leg broke again, and that was the end of Badger's brilliant career.

He later returned to Bramall Lane and remained part of the matchday hospitality team as recently as the start of the Covid lockdown. When former manager Chris Wilder – himself a boyhood Blade – took over at the club, Badger, along with his pals Tony Currie and Ted Hemsley, were consulted by the new boss.

Tragically, Len Badger, United's youngest ever captain, passed away on 20 May 2021, after a short illness. The club led the outpouring of grief felt by fans of all ages. Their emotional statement said that Badger could possibly have achieved greater success away from Bramall Lane, but that hadn't mattered to him. The most important thing to Len Badger was playing for Sheffield United. He was proud to be a Blade. The statement called Badger not only one of the club's greatest ever full-backs, but one of United's greatest characters.

It is normal for fans to pay tribute to a former player when he passes away, but the depth of pain felt by United fans seemed greater than the norm; like they had lost an actual friend. Current Blades skipper, Billy Sharp, wrote on Twitter: 'Devastated, my dad's all-time favourite Blades player, and somebody who I was lucky to share the two recent promotions with and got to shake his hand before every game. A wonderful man and player, thoughts to all Len's family.'

Former United defender, Kevin Gage, wrote, 'The word "legend" is bandied about quite often these days and has encroached into our vocabulary; therefore, the true meaning is lost occasionally. This man was and will always be an SUFC legend in the true sense of the word. RIP Mr LEN BADGER.'

Hundreds of fans also took to Twitter to offer their condolences and respect, many of them too young to have ever seen him play, but aware of his position in the club's fabric.

'RIP Len, I'm too young to have seen him play, but I've heard stories from my dad and uncles. What a player,' wrote one young fan.

Another United fan simply wrote, 'Heart-breaking news. You'll not meet a better man.'

Another regular at the Lane wrote, 'Devastating news, matchdays won't be the same.'

It was impossible to count the number of photographs of Len posing with fans at matchdays and other events shared on social media. His funeral procession was attended by hundreds of fans, silently paying their respects outside in the car park at Bramall Lane.

One ex-Blades favourite told me, 'There's a statue in that car park of a bloke that was more Wednesday than United. They should pull it down and have a statue of Len. He was all Sheffield United, through and through. No one deserves a statue at Bramall Lane more than Len Badger.'

Former captain Tony Kenworthy said, 'Kevin [McCabe] used to look after me. I'd bring the family to games three or four times a year, and they'd all be looked after. I used to leave my family and go and sit with Len. I just wanted to be around him. He was just a lovely, lovely bloke. We'd sit together talking, looking round the ground, and he'd say "Look at us, we're two lads off council estates and we've played over 1,000 games for this club between us Tony." I wanted to hug him. He was the only reason I went really, just to spend a couple of hours with Len. I loved him.'

Sadly for me personally – and you as a reader – I didn't get to speak to the man himself. Although he readily agreed to speak to me, pre-Covid, distancing rules and then, unfortunately, his ill health prevented the meeting taking place and alas, we all missed out.

With first Hemsley out of the team and now Badger, the defence was unfamiliar and hadn't played together very often. Cliff Calvert, signed from York City, came into the team alongside Garner, Bradford, Eddy and Colquhoun.

A 3-2 defeat at Derby County and draws against Middlesbrough and Newcastle United did little to expel the feeling of inevitability that United would be relegated well before the end of the season – the festive season.

On 3 January, United met Leicester City in the FA Cup third round. Sirrel decided to rest Chris Guthrie and gave a debut to young striker Keith Edwards. John Flynn replaced Calvert. Edwards was substituted after 64 minutes and Chris Garland scored a hat-trick for the Foxes as they were convincing 3-0 winners.

The youngsters trying to break into the squad – the likes of Edwards and Simon Stainrod – saw the team's poor form as an opportunity. With many of them playing in the reserves, and playing well, it was surely only a matter of time before they were called up for the first team.

United did enjoy a morale-boosting win in the County Cup over neighbours Wednesday at the Lane, but it would be Valentine's Day 1976 before Jimmy Sirrel eventually tasted his first league victory as Sheffield United manager, when the Blades beat Aston Villa 2-1: Woodward and Guthrie on target for the home side. United now had 13 points and were still ten points behind Burnley, 12 behind Wolves.

A 1-1 draw at Leicester City on 21 February gave cause for celebration, as United had remarkably avoided defeat two weeks in a row for the first time in recent memory. Three days later, they met relegation rivals Burnley at Turf Moor and Burnley opened the gap to 15 points, moving above Wolves on goal difference, after beating United 3-1.

A 0-0 draw against Queens Park Rangers gave United a point, but their trip to Maine Road ended in a 4-0 win for Manchester City. Johnstone scored his first goal for United at home to Wolves, but Wolves scored four.

The formality of United's relegation from the First Division was finally confirmed on 27 March, after they were thrashed 5-0 by Tottenham Hotspur. Simon Stainrod made his debut up front at White Hart Lane and another youngster, Tony Kenworthy, was an unused substitute.

Kenworthy had been in the party that travelled to Maine Road to face City, but didn't make the 12. In those days, Kenworthy was in digs on Donnington Road and would usually go home to his parents' house in Leeds on a Friday after training, and come back on the Saturday to play for the youth team. On the Friday night he received a phone call from the landlady on Donnington Road, saying the club were trying to contact him. He rang the manager and was told he was needed in Manchester the next day.

Kenworthy's dad drove him to Manchester and after finally managing to get parked, as he was trying to enter the players' entrance, he was stopped by security. 'I play for Sheffield United,' he told the guard, but the officer was having none of it. After three failed attempts, the guard finally agreed to call inside for one of the United staff to come and vouch for him. Cec Coldwell came and let him in.

He was fined £6 – a week's wages – for being late.

Kenworthy had signed for United while Ken Furphy was manager but had not been given a chance in the first team, even though he had captained the England youth team, playing alongside some very good players such as Kenny Sansom, Sammy Lee and recent Blades debutant, Stainrod. After being called to the Ball Inn training ground for a trial match following the defeat at Spurs, Kenworthy was given his first start at Norwich City.

He said, 'Twelve months before joining I'd been a ball boy at Leeds. You could see the Elland Road floodlights from my house. Furphy signed me but never fancied me, he just used to bollock me. Sirrel believed in me and gave me my chance. The senior players were great. I roomed with Eddie Colquhoun. He never spoke to me, I just followed him about like a schoolboy, but he looked after me on the pitch. He'd say to me during the game, "I'm going to chin you when we get back in that dressing room" – he never did though.

'He schooled me. You'd never get away with it these days, it'd be bullying, but it made me and I'm forever grateful to him. They all looked after me. Cec took me under his wing. He'd bollock me as well. When I wasn't feeling it, he'd say, "What's with the face? You've got a great job, you're at a great team. Don't you dare tell me you don't want it." All the older players were great. Your Ted Hemsley and Badger and Eddie Colquhoun. They all looked after me.

'There were some great characters at the club. I remember this old man who used to sweep the dressing rooms, stark bollock naked apart from his trainers. He used to talk to me.

I had no idea who he was. Somebody said to me one day, "Do you know who that is?" It was Harry Latham; he'd been there for nearly 50 years.'

With the pressure apparently lifted following the confirmation of relegation, United ran out 1-3 winners: Guthrie, Simon Stainrod and Currie all scored.

Kenworthy and Stainrod kept their places in the side to face West Ham United at Bramall Lane on 10 April. Stainrod scored again, as did Guthrie, after Woodward had scored the opener. United enjoyed a memorable 3-2 victory, only their fourth of the campaign, but their second in succession.

Away at Leeds United, four days later, on the Wednesday night, Leeds-born Kenworthy faced his hometown club, hoping to help the Blades to a third successive victory. The Leeds side included some big names: Trevor Cherry and Billy Bremner, the Gray brothers and Duncan McKenzie in attack; but the papers were talking about young Kenworthy and the Leeds legend, Norman Hunter.

Obvious comparisons were made between the two tough-tackling defenders, one a 17-year-old at the start of his career, one at the other end of his, having been part of England's World Cup-winning squad a decade earlier and the Leeds team that lost the European Cup Final in 1975.

The Blades employed tactics of soaking up the pressure in the hope of catching the talented Leeds side on the break. Kenworthy had a busy night, as did keeper Jim Brown – making several important saves to stay in the contest. The tactics worked. United recorded three consecutive wins for the first time all season, Alan Woodward scoring the only goal of the game. Kenworthy was rewarded with a booking after using all means possible to stop McKenzie.

The following week saw an abrupt end to the winning streak at Ayresome Park. A Tony McAndrew hat-trick for Middlesbrough made it a stroll for the home team. Kenworthy again got his name in the paper and the referee's notebook, after his challenge on David Mills broke the striker's collarbone. Although there was no malice from young Kenworthy, he could easily have been sent off for the tackle, even in those days.

The Blades recorded one more victory, away at Newcastle United, when Chris Guthrie scored the winner against his former club, but it was much too little, much too late.

The final game of the season saw Birmingham City come to Bramall Lane, needing a point for survival. United's fate had long been sealed, but if Birmingham got the point they needed, their neighbours Wolves would be relegated. United's player of the season Alan Woodward was presented his trophy before the game and celebrated by putting United ahead.

However, Birmingham got the point they needed when Terry Hibbitt equalised to send Wolves down. That goal was bitter-sweet in the Hibbitt family, as brother Kenny played for the relegated Wolves team.

Burnley separated Wolves and United and also dropped out of the division. Liverpool won the league with 60 points, pipping Queens Park Rangers to the title after beating sorry Wolves on the final day.

By the end of the season, United had accrued just 22 points, winning six of their 42 games. They lost ten games at Bramall Lane and 16 on the road. They conceded 82 goals in all and scored a dismal 33. Alan Woodward was United's top scorer, with ten. Guthrie scored nine. Another 13 were shared across the squad, and one was an own goal.

The ambition to have an arena fit for top-class football had ultimately cost United their place in the top division, much like it had Chelsea. The building of their stand played a crucial part in their fall from grace. By 1977, Chelsea's debts stood at close to £4m, and between 1974 and 1978, they failed to sign a single player.

United's failure to improve the squad and build on the previous season's fantastic results had also been costly. While it is arguable that United overachieved under Ken Furphy the previous season, it is certainly accurate to say that United underachieved this season.

Division One table 1975/76

	Played	*W*	*D*	*L*	*Points*
C Liverpool	42	23	14	5	60
2 QPR	42	24	11	7	59
3 Manchester United	42	23	10	9	56
22 **Sheffield United**	42	6	10	26	22

United manager 'Gentleman' John Harris 1973

The great Len Badger outjumps Howard Kendall 1972

Ted Hemsley and Tom McAlister thwart Trevor Francis 1972

Bill Dearden in action against Spurs 1973

Alan Woodward on the ball 1973 v Chelsea

Ken Furphy, United's tracksuit manager August 1975

Tony Currie takes on Liverpool's Steve Heighway

Mick Speight in 1975

Keith Edwards in 1976

Martin Peters in action for United 1980/81

Alejandro (Alex) Sabella

Young Blades striker Ian Benjamin (standing, first left) lines up for Len Cantello's historic blacks v whites game – May 1979

Chapter 12

IN THE aftermath of relegation, United faced financial disaster. With crippling loans and interest payments to be met, it was essential to sell more players, and even then, there would still be very little money to replace them.

Keith Eddy, Terry Garbett and Tony Field all headed to the North American Soccer League to join Pele at New York Cosmos under the supervision of Ken Furphy.

Cosmos were founded in 1970 by Ahmet and Nesuhi Ertegun with the financial backing of Warner Brothers president, Steve Ross. Cosmos were the marquee club of the NASL and were attracting massive crowds at their games. Before the forming of the NASL in 1968, football (or soccer as it was known there) struggled for popularity in the States. Huge investment poured into the league and Cosmos were the leading force, boosted by the signings of international superstars such as Brazilian legend Pele, German defender Franz Beckenbauer and Italian striker Giorgio Chinaglia.

Cosmos were one of the most glamorous teams in world football. Keith Eddy was named in the NASL's all-stars in his first season. After his playing career finished, he moved to

Canada, where he managed Toronto Blizzard. Tony Field later moved to Memphis Rogues in the American indoor league before finishing his career with New England Tea Men.

In June 1977 Cosmos attracted an NASL record crowd of 62,394 fans inside the Giants Stadium. They were treated to a hat-trick from 37-year-old Pele. He brought the curtain down on his magnificent career by leading Cosmos to the 1977 Soccer Bowl title. Following Pele's retirement, Cosmos' fortunes declined and so did the NASL. Viewing figures dropped and the league lost TV rights. The league eventually folded in 1985.

Forward Steve Cammack joined Len Badger at Chesterfield, keeper Tom McAlister was sold to Rotherham United, and Billy Dearden left for Chester and would also join Chesterfield a year later. But the most bitter pill to swallow for the Blades fans was the sale in June of the wonderful Tony Currie to Leeds United.

Currie was idolised at Bramall Lane, and decades later, as part of United's 120th anniversary year, he was named as United's greatest ever player. The new South Stand – the project that cost United their place in the First Division, and ultimately meant Currie's sale was inescapable – was renamed the Tony Currie Stand in his honour in 2018, a most fitting tribute.

Currie said at the time, 'I am overwhelmed by this honour; this is a very special tribute. Everyone knows what United and the club means to me – it's an unbreakable bond that began 50 years ago and is as strong today as it's ever been.'

In August 2018 TC was named as a director of the club. Co-owner at the time, Kevin McCabe said, 'This is great news. Like our manager [Chris Wilder] he is one of our own.'

In September 2019 though, when owner Kevin McCabe was ordered by a High Court judge to sell his share to Prince Abdullah, Currie announced he was stepping down from the Sheffield United board. Currie, who has for years held a football in the community role with the Blades, told the *Daily Mail*, 'It's a sad day for the club. Over the past 25 years Kevin has transformed this club.'

Legend is probably the most over-used word in football, but whether Currie's love affair with the club continues or not, he will always be remembered by the fans as an absolute legend. His sale to Leeds United brought a much-needed but insufficient £245,000 to United – just imagine what he would be worth in today's transfer market.

In 1970, former England World Cup hero Martin Peters (we will look at his role in United's history shortly) had been the subject of the first £200,000 British transfer fee. Kevin Keegan's transfer to Hamburg in 1977 raised twice Currie's fee for Liverpool. Keegan had been astute enough to have a £500k release clause included in his contract at Anfield, while Currie, who had recently signed a long-term deal with the Blades, was offloaded on the cheap by comparison. It would only be a couple more years before Britain saw its first £1 million player in Trevor Francis.

Currie would later play for QPR, where he captained the side in the FA Cup Final, conceding the penalty which won the game. He made 528 appearances during his club career, as well as playing for England on 17 occasions. He won 11 of those caps while at Leeds, yet it is widely believed he should have earned more caps, but Don Revie wasn't a fan. Alf Ramsey consistently picked Currie, as did Joe Mercer during his caretaker stint. It can't be coincidence that he didn't feature for the four years that Revie was in charge but did return after Revie's departure.

In Sheffield, Chris Guthrie led the attack in pre-season. He, new signing Ian 'Chico' Hamilton, Steve Ludlam, David Bradford and even Alan Woodward failed to score in five out of seven games. One was drawn, six were lost.

Despite winning none of their practice games, United fielded an unchanged team for the season opener, away at Luton Town. United failed to score again and were beaten 2-0.

Keith Edwards, who had made a handful of appearances the previous season, was brought into the side to partner Chris Guthrie for United's first home game in Division Two. On Tuesday, 24 August, 15,848 fans saw Edwards score his first senior goal for the Blades in a 2-2 draw with Wolves. Newcomer Hamilton also opened his account. Wolves had led 0-2 before Hamilton pulled one back. Edwards knocked in the equaliser – with what he describes as 'an absolute worldie', – from about five yards. It's not the sight of the ball hitting the net that Edwards recalls. 'The thing I remember, is saying to my girlfriend at the time, who later became my wife, that I couldn't believe the roar from the Kop. It was absolutely deafening. That's what sticks in my memory about that goal.'

On 30 August, more than 100 police officers were injured when the Notting Hill Carnival descended into a riot in the capital. Around 60 carnival-goers were also injured when violence erupted as police tried to arrest a pickpocket near Portobello Road. Several youths are reported to have gone to the pickpocket's aid, and soon the disturbance escalated. Over 60 people were arrested after police were attacked with stones and missiles.

The Blades drew 1-1 at home to Hereford United, Guthrie with United's goal. Colin Franks scored United's only goal in a 3-1 defeat to Chelsea in the League Cup. Three days later, United drew 1-1 at Southampton, United's 11th successive game, including pre-season, without a win.

Just over 13,500 were present when United finally did win. Ian Hamilton and Alan Woodward scored against Carlisle United at the Lane and an own goal from Carlisle's MacDonald made it 3-0 to the Blades.

On 17 September, a Friday night match, young Edwards scored his second for United in a 1-1 draw at Hull City. United drew the next game at home to Blackburn Rovers the following week. They had now won just one of their opening seven league games and were 14th in the table. New boss Sirrel had failed to impress the supporters so far.

Burnley were level on points with the Blades but had a worse goal difference, when they were beaten 1-0 at Bramall Lane on 2 October. Alan Woodward scored the second-half winner. A week later United faced Brian Clough's Nottingham Forest at the City Ground. A certain Terry Curran would play a massive part in the game.

After Ian Bowyer had opened the scoring on 11 minutes, Barry Butlin added a second. United pulled one back from the spot, scored by Chico Hamilton. Curran then went up a gear, making Forest's third goal, before going on a mazy run, evading the tackles of Garner, Ludlam and Calvert then playing a one-two with Viv Anderson to finish the move and make it 4-1. Curran then turned provider, playing in Peter Withe for Forest's fifth. It was Curran again who started the move that resulted in Viv Anderson's first ever goal for Forest, making it 6-1.

The visit of Fulham on 16 October 1976 included another gifted individual: even if slightly past his prime, George Best was in their line-up, and brought almost 29,000 to the Lane, the highest home gate of the season. However, the big, excited crowd and the mercurial Mr Best failed to inspire the Blades (or Fulham), and the match ended 1-1.

Some senior players were now starting to lose confidence in the manager and his style, and there was certainly dissent within the ranks. The older players were constantly on at the boss to give the youngsters a chance. An away trip to Charlton Athletic would see United score twice but the home team scored three. Simon Stainrod, a Sheffield lad, who after breaking into the first team the previous year and scoring twice, replaced the declining Johnstone for the trip to Ninian Park, was rewarded with another two goals, as United beat Cardiff City 0-2. Teenager Gary Hamson made his debut and had a hand in both goals. Tony Kenworthy, who had lost his place to Colin Calvert after the Forest defeat, returned to the team.

Debutant Hamson had almost signed apprenticeship forms with Nottingham Forest, but recalls, 'Brian Clough insisted on meeting all the parents before he signed anyone as an apprentice. On the day we were all due to sign, I was in hospital with a knee injury. When I recovered, I thought I'd missed my chance. Clough was away on holiday and I played in a Nottinghamshire Youth League game, for Ilkeston Town. I scored a hat-trick in the game, against Mansfield.

'I heard after the game that Jimmy Sirrel's scout had been watching. Me and my parents travelled to Sheffield and on the Sunday they took us all out for Sunday dinner. I signed on Monday. I played in the Central League for the reserves.

We played at Leeds and drew 2-2. As I was sat on the bus to go home, a man got on and came and told me I'd had a great game. I had no idea who he was, but the manager got on the bus and gave the man a hug. When the stranger got off the bus, the boss told me it was John Charles. Bloody hell, that guy had played for Juventus. I was told on the Friday night that I was playing on Saturday against Cardiff.'

Hamson was only 16 when he signed, and he shared digs with Tony Kenworthy. One might think there was a split camp with a growing group of youngsters, but Hamson recalls them all being one big happy group. The senior players and the youngsters all mixed and got on well.

At home to Notts County at the start of November, United – including three teenagers – completed back-to-back wins for the first time. Chris Guthrie scored the only goal and United moved up to seventh in the league. The win was possibly one with mixed emotions for Sirrel, putting one over his former employers.

A 0-1 defeat at Blackpool, and a 1-1 draw with Orient, in which Keith Edwards scored, were followed by another two successive victories. Alan Woodward scored in the 0-1 win at Millwall, and Chico Hamilton scored the penalty that would beat league leaders, Chelsea, at the Lane on 3 December.

One other win in December, along with a draw and two defeats, saw United slip a place in the league to eighth at the turn of the year. The first game of 1977 was a goalless affair in the FA Cup third round against Newcastle United.

Also, at the turn of the year, record label EMI fired the Sex Pistols because of their shocking public behaviour. Following their appearance on Bill Grundy's *Today* programme on TV, where the band repeatedly used foul language, EMI announced that they were unable to promote the group's records, in view of the adverse publicity generated over the past two months. The final straw apparently was the group spitting at each other while waiting to catch a plane at Heathrow and using abusive language to staff. The Pistols were only three months into the deal and had released one single, 'Anarchy in the UK'. In March, the band signed for A&M records, but by June had been sacked by them also.

Paul Garner netted in the FA Cup replay at St James' Park, but the Blades were beaten 3-1. United were winless in February, drawing two and losing two. By the time they met Blackburn Rovers on 5 March, United had slipped to 16th in the league. Ted Hemsley, who hadn't played a league game for nearly 70 weeks – his previous game being on 8 November 1975 – returned to the side, but the 1-0 defeat at Ewood Park would be his last appearance for United.

He had been at the club for over nine years, playing in 247 league games, and had been an important part of the team that had been promoted to the First Division in 1971 and one of the stars of the team that so nearly challenged for a place in Europe. On leaving the Blades he spent two seasons at Doncaster Rovers, before retiring. In a 20-year career, he played more than 500 games. Like his great friend, Len Badger, Hemsley has been part of the matchday experience since Chris Wilder returned to the club.

He continued to play cricket professionally for a further three years after hanging up his boots. His impressive cricket career spanned three decades, seeing him feature in 243 first-class matches for Worcestershire and score 9,740 runs. Had it not been for his football career, Hemsley would undoubtedly have played cricket for England. Bob Willis, the legendary England bowler said, 'There's no telling how far Ted might have gone in cricket if soccer had not claimed his attention for a decade or so. He certainly always looked a well-organised batsman – sensible, brave, with the judgement to use his shots when necessary.'

He was certainly brave – steadfastly refusing to wear a helmet when batting.

In 1982, he was awarded a benefit year. Many top sports personalities from around the world lined up to pay tribute,none more so than the man who had managed him twice – Arthur Rowley. He wrote at the time, 'Ted, as always, led by example and I soon made him captain at Shrewsbury. When I left for Sheffield United, Ted was to be one of my first signings as I knew he would rise to the challenge.'

Ian Porterfield summed up Ted perfectly when he said, 'To play any sport at a professional level requires a great deal of talent, dedication and hard work, but for a player to be successful at two of the major professional games played in this country, he must have something a little bit extra.'

The Blades bounced back from the loss at Blackburn three days later, at home to Cardiff City. Keith Edwards scored his fifth of the season after Woodward had put the hosts in front. Teenager Gary Hamson scored his first goal for the club to make it 3-0.

In the next home game, new signing John Cutbush started at right-back. Maltese-born Cutbush began his career as a 15-year-old apprentice at Spurs, although he never made a senior appearance for them. At the age of 22, he signed for Fulham, making 134 appearances, including one in the 1975 FA Cup Final.

Keith Edwards scored both goals, as United took some revenge on Nottingham Forest for the thrashing earlier in the season. The 2-0 win moved United back up to 13th in Division Two. Edwards was marked during the game by former Liverpool player Larry Lloyd, but gave him the run-around with ease. The *Mirror* reported, 'Edwards, 20-year-old striker, struggling to establish himself as a regular member of United's first team, felled Forest with a double blow. He scored both goals and tore the Forest defence apart.'

Edwards remembers Kenny Burns playing at the back for Forest, and recalls giving Forest manager Clough a cheeky wink after scoring his second.

United then travelled to Hereford United, with Edwards on a fantastic run of form. He scored both the Blades' goals for the second time in four days in the 2-2 draw. Edwards scored his fifth in three games at Craven Cottage, but Fulham won the game 3-2. Edwards then scored in the defeat at Notts County, scored two in a 3-0 win over Charlton Athletic, one in the victory over Oldham Athletic, another in the win at Bolton Wanderers and completed the sequence with the consolation goal in a 1-5 thumping at Blackpool. It was Edwards's 11th goal in eight games. Despite still sitting mid-table, his goals had given United and their fans what they very much needed – a new hero.

Edwards scored two more before the end of the season and United finished in 11th place. Edwards was often perceived as arrogant and ultra cocky, but says it was just his way of dealing with the pressure. 'Looking back, it was a bit embarrassing at times, in hindsight – what was I thinking? I remember Tony Pritchett being on our team bus and asking me a question about scoring. Tony loved the old guard – I think it was three years before he gave me a man of the match. I said "it's not a question of if I score, it's just which half I'm going to score in". I've no idea why I said that. I think it was just my way of hiding the shyness.'

Wolves were champions, eventually finishing two points ahead of Chelsea, and Nottingham Forest finished third. Manchester United won the FA Cup, beating Arsenal 2-1, and Liverpool won the First Division title. Spurs were relegated along with Sunderland and Stoke City.

Carlisle United, Plymouth Argyle and Hereford United were relegated from Division Two. Wednesday finished eighth in Division Three.

Keith Edwards scored 18 goals in 36 games in all competitions, a more than decent return for a young lad in his first full season. At one point during the season, he scored 14 in 11 games. Alan Woodward – by then 30 years old – played in all but two of United's league games, scoring ten goals.

Results had been indifferent, including two notable thrashings, and fans had hoped for better than an 11th-place finish, but the emergence of some talented young players who established themselves in the team – Tony Kenworthy, Keith Edwards, Simon Stainrod and 17-year-old Gary Hamson – had all been positives. They were a close group, and all got along with each other. There was healthy competition – they all thought they were better than the others, but they respected each other. They had been brought up through the ranks around players like Currie, Woodward, Eddy and Colquhoun and had to respect them.

Manager Sirrel blamed the poor form on his senior players – even though he had hardly used some of them, which did little to heal the growing rift. Most of the players disliked Sirrel's training methods, which still mainly consisted of practice matches, day in, day out.

Sirrel added more youth, buying 21-year-old Irish attacker Bobby Campbell for £10,000 from Huddersfield Town. Campbell, described by one of his team-mates as 'a lovely lad but bloody scary', started his career at Aston Villa, where he made just ten appearances for the first team, before being shipped out on loan to Halifax and then sold to Huddersfield.

Steve Ludlam was sold to Carlisle United. Ludlam, a Chesterfield lad, had joined United in 1973 and worked his way into the team in 1975. He struggled to earn a regular place in the side and started 27 games in a United shirt. He made 96 appearances for Carlisle, before becoming Chester's record signing in 1980 for a fee of £45,000. He ended his first season at Chester as their top goalscorer with seven goals. He later moved abroad and played in Finland, but injury ended his career and he retired at the age of 28.

Chris Guthrie was sold to Swindon Town for £20,000. He played 60 games for the Blades, scoring 15 times. The striker had spent two years at Bramall Lane and lost £80,000 in value. His goals per game ratio improved slightly after leaving United. In 45 appearances for Swindon, he netted 12 times.

In 1978 he moved to Fulham, where he scored 15 in 50 games, before a brief spell at Millwall. A poll of United fans showed Guthrie never really managed to win them over, despite scoring a few memorable goals.

Twitter user @RanmoorBlade lamented, 'Tommy Docherty said of us when we signed him [Guthrie], if you buy third division players, that's where you'll end up.'

The 1977/78 season began in front of 1,975 fans at Plainmoor, home of Torquay United. Bobby Campbell scored on his debut, as his new side drew 1-1. The Devon air must have agreed with him, as the 22-mile trip to Exeter's St James Park for the second friendly resulted in him grabbing two more as United won 4-1, Edwards and Hamilton scoring the other two.

On 16 August, the world mourned the death of Elvis Presley. Presley, aged just 42, was discovered slumped in the bathroom of his Graceland mansion in Memphis. Initial post-mortem findings revealed the singer had died from a heart attack. Dr Francisco, who carried out the examination, said there were no signs of any other disease or drug abuse. The day after the star's death, thousands of fans filed past his body, which lay in state. Despite Dr Francisco's finding it was heavily rumoured at the time that Elvis's death was due to a cocaine addiction and regular use of other drugs. In the years after his death, his overindulgences and addictions were well documented. He had spent 386 weeks in the UK top ten. He hit number one 21 times. In 2020, over 40 years after his premature death, Presley's net worth was estimated at $300 million.

The new Division Two season started on 20 August 1977 – the day NASA launched Voyager 2. United were away at newly relegated Tottenham Hotspur. Keith Edwards and new strike partner Campbell started up front. Spurs beat United 4-2, Hamilton and Edwards scoring for the Blades.

The first home game of the season saw Hull City visit the Lane for a Tuesday night game; new partnership Edwards and Campbell got a goal each as United won 2-0. The following Saturday, though, the same team lost 2-1 away at Bolton Wanderers, Woodward with his first of the season for United.

A League Cup second-round tie took United to Goodison Park. Paul Garner, suffering the effects of a serious car crash, was absent. Kenworthy returned to the side after being on the bench for recent games. The Toffees were too good and beat United comfortably, 3-0.

Keith Edwards scored again in the 1-1 draw at Sunderland's Roker Park, but neither Edwards nor United could score in the next three games – all were defeats, and the Blades conceded nine goals. The third of those games saw the return of Geoff Salmons on loan.

Away at Brighton and Hove Albion, United lost for a fourth successive game, this time 2-1. It was a disastrous start, with one win and five defeats, and United were languishing in 21st position in Division Two. On 28 September, Jimmy Sirrel and the board parted company and Blades legend Cec Coldwell, now a coach at the club, took over as caretaker manager. Within a month, Sirrel returned to Notts County, who were themselves struggling for survival in Division Two. He remained there until 1982, by which time he had guided them back to the top flight.

He was in charge again in 1985 and has a stand named after him at their Meadow Lane ground. After leaving Meadow Lane, he took up a scouting role at Derby. He died in 2008, aged 86. When asked once why Jimmy was never at home, his wife was quoted as saying, 'Well, you can't cage a tiger.'

October saw an upturn in fortunes, with United finally able to win two games in a row. Gary Hamson, Alan Woodward and Keith Edwards all scored in the 3-2 victory over Southampton, and Edwards grabbed a couple more goals in the 4-1 defeat of Sirrel's Notts County. Campbell scored his second for the club and youngster Hamson converted a penalty.

United then drew at Mansfield Town and Millwall, with a victory at home to Burnley sandwiched between them. United went into the home game with Fulham unbeaten in five games under caretaker Coldwell. It was Fulham that took the lead, but Bobby Campbell got to the dead-ball line and his deep cross was met by a bullet header from Ian Hamilton to level. Woodward added a second from the edge of the box, to ensure the Blades claimed victory.

Campbell scored in the next two games when United drew at Blackpool and beat Oldham Athletic, rising to eighth in the table. A defeat at Charlton Athletic and a draw with Bristol Rovers halted the ascent.

Away at Cardiff City on 3 December, Simon Stainrod was preferred to Keith Edwards, who hadn't scored in eight games. Despite doing well after breaking into the team the previous season, this was Stainrod's first start of the campaign. Bobby Campbell, the player who had previously kept Stainrod out of the team, scored two; Colin Calvert, Tony Kenworthy, Ian Hamilton and Alan Woodward also scored as United put six past the Welshmen. Woodward's goal was his 150th in the league for the club.

Four days later, at home to Blackburn Rovers, Hamilton picked up a loose ball and went on a swerving run, before beautifully placing it into the corner for 1-0. Woodward added a second to confirm the win. Woodward scored two more on Boxing Day as his side beat Orient 2-0.

Keith Edwards returned to the side on New Year's Eve, to partner Stainrod against Hull City. Edwards picked the ball up out wide on the left and delivered an inch-perfect cross for Stainrod to head in his first goal of the season.

Later, Edwards latched on to a Longhorn through-ball to end his barren run, tucking the ball under the advancing keeper with the confidence of a striker on top of his form. Late in the second half, Woodward fed Stainrod on the right, who cut inside and drove a left-footed shot into the corner for his second of the game.

January, though, was disappointing and while goals from Keith Edwards and Gary Hamson earned a draw against Spurs, United lost three on the bounce, conceding five goals in each game, including a thrashing by Arsenal in the cup, a game in which Chico Hamilton missed a penalty.

After the third game in which United had shipped five goals, away at Sunderland, it was time to look for a more suitable and more permanent replacement for Sirrel than Cec Coldwell.

Chapter 13

ON 26 January 1978, Harry Haslam arrived from Luton Town, where he had steered the Hatters from the Fourth Division to the First. At Kenilworth Road he had some very capable coaches including David Pleat and Danny Bergara, and the latter joined him at United.

Haslam had been in great demand. Millwall had offered him a five-year contract to take over the vacant manager's role at The Den, and he had been linked with a scouting role at Old Trafford, where he had served as an apprentice, due to his impressive reputation for finding talented players.

While in his first role as a manager, at Welsh non-league side Barry Town, Haslam had amazed the footballing world by somehow managing to acquire the signatures of two Swedish internationals – Bengt Berndtsson, who would play close to 600 games for Gothenburg, and keeper Sven Lindberg. Berndtsson had 29 international caps, and just months after representing Sweden in the 1958 World Cup, Haslam and chairman John Baily miraculously persuaded the winger to join tiny Barry Town on loan. Not only could Haslam find players, but he was also a shrewd businessman. It was reported that he saved Luton from going under, reducing their debts by £500,000. It has also been suggested that in the days before agents, Haslam would often negotiate himself a tidy share of the deals he brokered.

United undoubtedly needed inspiration in the team, and still with little cash to spend, Haslam appeared to fit the bill perfectly. However, his methods were somewhat of a culture shock for the United players. They had grown used to the tracksuit manager's approach – daily practice matches, supervised closely by the boss. Now they were coached by Danny Bergara, and Haslam rarely – if ever – appeared at the training ground. He preferred to focus on running things from afar, then to pop into the dressing room on matchday and wish his team well, safe in the knowledge that his trusted assistant Bergara had the team well drilled. Bergara, for his part, was a brilliant coach who believed in playing attractive, technical football.

Bergara had been a striker in his playing days, moving to Spain when he was 20 to play for Real Mallorca, where he was top scorer for four seasons. While playing in Spain, Bergara married an English travel guide. When his playing career finished, the couple came to live in England. One of Bergara's cousins was one of Harry Haslam's many acquaintances and the then Luton boss appointed Bergara to the role of youth-team coach.

It is widely understood that the Uruguayan was years ahead of his time. Whether he was ahead of United's time remained to be seen. His methods certainly differed greatly to those of the previous regime. Sirrel had insisted on resolute, hard work – one might say unsophisticated football – but Bergara had more tricks and skills than most of the senior players at the club. Suddenly, training was about learning techniques such as curling and bending the ball, which delighted some of the younger players, who were eager to improve. It's no stretch to suggest that the coach was a better footballer, technically, than any of the players. Young striker Edwards rated Bergara very highly. 'One of the most disappointing things in football for me was the coaches. I learned more from my dad than I learned from most of the coaches, but Danny was brilliant. I actually learned from him. He and Haslam told me I was the next Malcolm Macdonald. I was happy with that.'

United failed to record a win throughout the whole of February, losing both league games and a friendly against Southern League Hastings United. It was March 1978 – over a month after Haslam's arrival – before United returned to winning ways, against Mansfield Town. A long ball from Ian Hamilton found Keith Edwards loitering on the edge of the six-yard box. The striker turned on the spot to wrong-foot the keeper, before sticking the ball in the top corner of the empty net in the fourth minute. Woodward thrashed in a second in the last minute, putting the game to bed.

Simon Stainrod scored a consolation goal in a 4-1 defeat at Burnley in the next game, and Colin Franks did the same in a 1-2 defeat at home to Stoke City. Stainrod was on the scoresheet again on 18 March, when United put five past Millwall. Bobby Campbell scored twice, Alan Woodward converted a penalty and Mick Speight scored one in the 5-2 win.

Stainrod, Speight and Woodward all scored again in the 4-1 victory over Haslam's former employers, Luton Town, towards the end of March. Speight scored his third goal in less than three weeks in the 2-0 success over Brighton and

Hove Albion, John Cutbush being the unlikely contributor of the second.

Edwards found his scoring boots again to net the winner against Charlton Athletic and in the 2-1 win away at Notts County, while Woodward scored his 12th of the campaign in United's last victory of the season. The Blades went down 0-1 to Cardiff City at Bramall Lane in the last fixture of the campaign. Just 13,687 fans were there.

United's respectable finish to the season helped attain a 12th-place finish with 40 points: one place lower than the previous season but with the same number of points.

Despite progress stalling, and the shocking start to the season, some of the youngsters were now showing real potential. Midfielder Gary Hamson had established himself in the first team, Simon Stainrod had only scored six goals in 24 games, but was playing well, Bobby Campbell had scored 11 in his first season and Keith Edwards had scored 16 in all competitions. The partnership between Stainrod and Edwards was an exciting prospect. Both were talented for sure and had different styles that complemented each other. Stainrod was something of a maverick, had the tricks and liked to beat an opponent. Like Edwards, he was often considered arrogant, but those who played with him said he was a lovely lad too. Edwards was more direct and just wanted to score, more than anything else. Given the chance to flourish, both players believed they had the makings of a great partnership.

Under the guidance of Bergara (with observations from Haslam), United fans were looking forward to a summer of progress. It seemed inevitable that Haslam would make changes to the squad. It was clear that the team needed strengthening if the Blades were to mount a serious challenge to return to the top division.

A decision by the EEC (European Economic Community) in February 1978 had effectively ruled that the country of a player's birth should not dictate his ability to play sports in any country. In the summer the annual general meeting of the Football League decided to lift its de facto ban on foreign players taking part in our beautiful game.

It is true of course, that long before 1978, there were notable exceptions to a largely British league. In addition to the aforementioned Swedes, there were other foreign imports. The great Bert Trautmann for example, signed for Manchester City after being held in England as a prisoner of war, and played for City throughout the 1950s and early 60s. The German famously broke his neck during the 1956 FA Cup Final. Before that, Karl Aage Hansen played for Huddersfield Town and Viggo Jensen played for Hull City after representing Denmark at the 1948 London Olympics. The very first foreign player in England is widely accepted to have been Canadian Walter Bowman, who turned out for Accrington as far back as the late 1800s.

In 1929 United were attracting talent from abroad. Full-back John 'Jock' Gibson, who was born in Philadelphia, signed for the Blades from Hull City for £5,000. The American played 74 games for United before moving to Luton Town in 1933. Gibson would make just three appearances for the Hatters before going to work at the Vauxhall plant in the city. He later played for Vauxhall Motors.

Haslam, with that reputation for dealing and finding new talent, generated some excitement among fans by casting his net further afield than they were used to. In that summer of 1978, the world was hooked as Argentina beat Holland in the World Cup Final and TV audiences were thrilled by the tickertape confetti that was strewn across the pitch in Buenos Aires, as Mario Kempes scored his two goals. In the Argentine side was the diminutive Osvaldo Ardiles, and Haslam had earmarked him as a potential signing before the tournament but apparently had a change of heart on the way there. Tottenham would eventually bring him and fellow countryman Ricardo Villa to England, after Haslam phoned the Spurs boss Keith Burkinshaw to alert him to their talents.

While Haslam and Bergara were scouting, they spotted a teenager playing for Argentinos Juniors called Diego Maradona. Haslam had all but agreed a £150,000 deal for Maradona – it has been claimed that the deal was so close to completion that the plane tickets were even booked – but despite Haslam's best efforts, and with costs suddenly rising to £400,000, fuelled by agents and others, the board got cold feet and at the last minute the youngster decided to stay in Argentina.

It would be remiss to not discuss here the numerous stories, myths and tales surrounding the Maradona saga. Many of you will have been shaking your head in disagreement at the previous paragraph. There are endless versions of what really happened. One such tale claims that just as Haslam was about to capture the signature of the man who would become the best footballer in the world, the country's notoriously bent military police got wind of the deal and wanted a piece of the action. It has been claimed that they turned up at Haslam's hotel room and demanded £150,000 for their own pockets, or Maradona wouldn't be allowed to leave the country. The money apparently wasn't an issue, but the thought of bribery was. Either the board wasn't brave enough, or Haslam wasn't, but either way, they decided not to pursue the deal further.

There are countless other versions of the story, which are equally entertaining. One thing that is irrefutable is that Maradona did go on to be a magnificent footballer. He is adjudged by many to have been one of, if not the greatest football player of all time. His colourful and controversial career saw him play for some of the world's biggest clubs.

He had been at Argentinos since he was eight years old, making his league debut at the age of 15. In 167 appearances for them, he scored 115 goals. He played for them until 1981, when he signed for Boca Juniors for $4million. He scored twice on his Boca debut. After the 1982 World Cup, Maradona was sold to Barcelona, for a then world record fee of £5m. Despite his time there being marred by injuries and off-field incidents, he played 36 games for the Spanish side, scoring an impressive 22 goals.

By 1984, Maradona was reaching his peak and he moved to Italian giants Napoli, with 85,000 fans turning out to greet him on his arrival in Naples. Despite his career being riddled with controversy and hindered by many well-documented drug issues, he played just under 500 club games in total. He represented his country 91 times, scoring 34 goals, including at least one, famously, with his hand.

He later went on to manage the Argentina national side, as well as being in charge of half a dozen clubs. In later years, after decades of drink and drug abuse, Maradona's health deteriorated. In November 2020, Maradona was admitted to hospital with unspecified psychological problems. He was released ten days later, but on 25 November, aged just 60, he suffered a fatal heart attack.

An investigation found that his death would have been preventable with proper care. The investigation continues at the time of writing this.

Haslam moved his attention to a 23-year-old midfielder, Alejandro Javier Sabella. Sabella had been at River Plate for four years, during which time they had won both of Argentina's major domestic trophies in 1975 and 1977. Uruguayan-born coach Bergara had to act as interpreter as Sabella spoke little English and Haslam spoke less Spanish.

Sabella had acquired several nicknames in Buenos Aires, one of which was 'Pachorra', which crudely translated to 'the sluggish one'. Another of his nicknames was 'El Mago' which meant 'the magician'. River Plate eventually sold the midfielder to Haslam for £160,000 (a fee which included a vast chunk of the gate receipts from a game to be played between the two clubs later).

Veteran ITV commentator, John Helm, was on duty in Argentina before the World Cup, during the preparations. He recalls a game between River Plate and Belgrano being used as a practice run for the TV companies to get the technology right. He told me that Sabella, while not in the national team, was the outstanding player in that game and shone above the rest of the players with his skill and flair as he repeatedly embarked on dazzling dribbles, feigning and dropping a shoulder as he glided past his opponents.

Other foreign players would also come to England that summer. Along with Sabella and his fellow countrymen, Ardiles and Villa, Alberto Tarantini signed for Birmingham City. Fiery defender Tarantini was the youngest of Argentina's successful World Cup squad but shortly before the competition he had a contractual falling-out with his club, Boca Juniors, and found himself without a club. Boca were a powerful force in Argentina and exerted pressure on other clubs in the country not to sign him. Birmingham boss Jim Smith spent £295,000 on the player but his time in England was short-lived, and he is probably best remembered for a brutal challenge on Brian Greenhoff, and for punching a supporter.

Ipswich Town manager Bobby Robson bought Arnold Muhren from Twente for £150,000 and a year later bought his former team-mate, Frans Thijssen. Over the next few years many more foreign players would grace our game.

On returning to England with his new purchase, Harry Haslam surprised United fans by selling 21-year-old Keith Edwards to Third Division Hull City for £55,000. There had been reports of bids up to and even above £200,000, so the fee was a little disappointing – not least to Edwards himself, who was expecting ten per cent of a bigger fee. Edwards says, 'I remember saying to my dad, "he must not like Malcolm Macdonald".'

Edwards told the papers at the time, 'At first my heart said no, but then my brain said yes. I thought about Hull and decided the move could be good for me. After all, I think they'll win more than they lose. And they've got Wilf McGuinness.' In reality, Edwards was hurt by the move. United's willingness to sell him, and for a relatively small fee, made Edwards determined to succeed for his new club. If United didn't want him, he didn't want to be there.

He hoped Wilf McGuinness would help him develop further. 'Wilf was a strange chap – humorous. Not sure I learned much though. I used to just annoy him because I answered back. He had me by the throat one day in training. He's had a dodgy ticker as well. I did develop though, not because of coaches, just because my body developed, and my game developed.'

Over the next three years Edwards blossomed from a potentially great goalscorer to an actual great goalscorer. He scored 57 times in 132 games for the Tigers, including one against Wednesday and a couple against United. In his first season for Hull, Edwards scored 24 goals. Fans who replied to a recent survey voted the sale of Edwards as the worst sale of any Sheffield United player, including the earlier sale of Tony Currie. Edwards would later return triumphantly, but that chapter will be in the next book.

More players would leave the club, and surprisingly, more would arrive, in contrast to the last few years of no spending. Striker Bobby Campbell was given a free transfer and signed briefly for Vancouver Whitecaps, but joined Huddersfield Town for a second time soon after. He would later enjoy two spells at Bradford City, where he became their all-time top scorer. John Flynn, who cost United £5,000 in 1969, was given a free transfer to neighbours Rotherham United.

There was talk of Tony Kenworthy leaving for Watford but after a decent pre-season, Haslam decided to keep the defender. Steve Finnieston was bought from Chelsea for around £90,000 before Edwards was sold. Finnieston had signed for Chelsea as a 12-year-old boy but didn't break into the first team until 1976/77 when he scored 24 goals.

Haslam gambled further with United's finances, buying John Matthews from First Division Arsenal for £90,000. Matthews had spent four seasons at Highbury, making 45 appearances. When he joined the Gunners as an apprentice, Matthews was a defender but later moved to a midfield role. With the likes of Graham Rix and Liam Brady for competition, and an absence from the side with a broken leg, Matthews found it difficult to become a regular. He boasted an explosive shot though, and could pass a ball, as well as being able to hold his own in a tackle. He could also take penalties.

Haslam's new star player, Alex Sabella, made his Sheffield United debut against Orient on 19 August 1978. Blades fans also got their first look at new striker, Finnieston. Haslam was watching his new charges from the stand, dishing out instructions on the phone to Bergara in the dug-out.

Fans had spent hours tearing up newspaper to throw on to the pitch to emulate the scenes in the World Cup for their first sight of Alejandro Sabella – even if most of them couldn't pronounce his name. Of course, this being pre-internet, no one really knew what to expect from the little Argentinian, but the mere fact that he was Argentinian, and they had just won the World Cup, meant he had to be something special. Add in a few slightly exaggerated statements from master spin doctor Haslam about Sabella's previous achievements, and excitement and expectation were high.

Sabella's first meaningful contribution was to take a corner, which found Simon Stainrod's head for the opener inside the first five minutes. A mistake from Tony Kenworthy let in Joe Mayo to level for Orient with a rasping drive, past the helpless Steve Conroy. Mexborough-born Peter Kitchen spoiled the party further, when he made it 1-2 with a near-post header five minutes before half-time. The scores stayed that way and the majority of the 19,000 fans that turned up, left disappointed.

An early-season, midweek trip to Leicester City four days later brought United's first win of the campaign, and new signing John Matthews scored the winner. Sabella scored his first goal for his new team the following Saturday in a 2-2 draw with Preston North End. Stainrod scored the other.

So, it had been a balanced start: played three, lost one, won one, drawn one; but positively, two of Haslam's new signings had scored already.

Kenyan President Jomo Kenyatta died peacefully in his sleep on 22 August. Kenyatta, 89, who had led the country since its independence in 1963 and was widely regarded as Father of the Nation, had made a public appearance the previous day. Still revered today, there is a public holiday in his honour in Kenya each October.

On 28 August 1978, European champions Liverpool came to Bramall Lane in the League Cup. Two days earlier Liverpool had beaten Manchester City 4-1, with goals from Graham Souness, Kenny Dalglish and Alan Kennedy. Before that they'd beaten Ipswich Town convincingly 3-0 and had beaten Queens Park Rangers in the opening game of the season.

Tony Kenworthy was ruled out with a knee injury that he had sustained in the Preston game. Andy Keeley came in to partner Matthews at the back. Keeley had joined at the turn of the year on a free transfer from Spurs after failing to establish himself in their team.

Gary Hamson had also picked up a knock in the draw with Preston, but despite just two days' recovery – the Liverpool game was on Monday night – Hamson was deemed fit enough to play. He was given the role of man-marking the great Terry McDermott. The average age of the United team that night was 23. Hamson had turned 18 just four days earlier. It's a cliché we often hear pundits use when they talk about young players being fearless. Hamson wasn't fazed by marking McDermott: 'McDermott's game was all about running. He'd get up and down the pitch all game, but I knew I was probably the fittest in our team, so I didn't mind. Speighty was marking Souness, and I took McDermott.'

As expected, the best team in the continent were by far the better side; one report said their first-half performance looked as though the Reds thought they only needed to turn up to beat United.

Alan Woodward almost upset the bookies when he latched on to a Gary Hamson cross but managed to put his effort the wrong side of the post. At a United free kick, referee Mr Lloyd booked the entire Liverpool wall – Terry McDermott, Jimmy Case, Phil Neal and Kenny Dalglish – for refusing to retreat.

In the second half, Liverpool continued to dominate the game. John Matthews cleared a Steve Heighway effort off the line, and John Cutbush cleared a goal-bound effort from Graeme Souness. Dalglish hit the post, only to see his effort roll agonisingly along the line and Steve Conroy in the United goal, possibly having the game of his career, made some outstanding saves to keep the Blades in the tie.

Ten minutes from time, Alex Sabella and Colin Franks fought for the ball in the Liverpool area, and when it broke free to Hamson, he took a touch, moving the ball to his left. He then drove it towards goal, curling it just inside the post, to send the Blades players into a heap in front of the John Street Stand, with the home fans delirious.

The *Liverpool Echo* reported the following day, 'When Sheffield United's 18-year-old midfield lad Gary Hamson drove a perfect shot past Ray Clemence to knock Liverpool out of the League Cup last night, he set up a shock wave of disbelief which must have swept through football. For a Second Division team to beat a side which, in thrashing Ipswich and Manchester City last week had looked well nigh unbeatable, was a result which qualified for the "can you believe it?" routine. The four-way caution for the Liverpool wall was as astonishing as the fact that United won.'

The goal would be Hamson's proudest moment in football. Liverpool beat Spurs 7-0 the following week and went on to win the First Division title by a mile at the end of the season, amassing a record 68 points.

United's next game, just two days later, was the one arranged to offset the cost of bringing Sabella to Sheffield. Over 22,000 fans attended and United lost 1-2 at Bramall Lane to a very impressive River Plate team that included Argentina captain, Daniel Passarella. Jim Brown made a rare appearance in goal, but otherwise it was the same team that had beaten the magnificent Liverpool. Woodward scored a penalty for the Blades, which turned out to be his last goal for United, but after the colossal effort against Liverpool, it's perhaps little wonder that the Argentinians won.

Back to domestic football, and Haslam's heroes went down 2-0 at Selhurst Park. A week later, they lost by the same margin away at Fulham, in front of a mere 6,672 inside Craven Cottage. At the Cottage, Alan Woodward played his final competitive game in a United shirt, after 536 matches and 158 goals in 16 years. He had joined the Blades as a 17-year-old in 1963, making his debut in 1964. He left as the club's post-war record goalscorer. How he was overlooked by multiple England managers is bizarre and frankly scandalous. His explosive shot with either foot had scored goals in the top two tiers of English football for a decade and a half, yet he never got the recognition, outside of Sheffield, that he deserved. He was feared from dead-ball situations, and few could compete with his ability to cross the ball. Woodward had even stood in as goalkeeper in pre-substitute days, conceding just once in over 150 minutes between the sticks.

Player of the year four times, he played alongside some of United's greatest icons – Currie, Badger, Hemsley, the Shaws, Mick Jones, Keith Edwards: he had played with all of them, and is still considered by many Blades fans as one of the best.

In 1978, at the age of 32, he was headed to Tulsa Roughnecks to join the rapidly expanding overseas contingent playing in the NASL. Tony Currie described him as the greatest he ever played with. Woodward played 47 games in America, where he was nicknamed Boomer.

His former manager John Harris once said, 'Alan simply has no concept of how much talent he has.'

On retiring from football in 1981, Woodward settled in Tulsa. He lived there until he passed away in May 2015, aged 68.

He played one last time for the Blades in a testimonial for W R Rogers of Norton Woodseats FC on 12 September 1978, before jetting off to the States.

Former team-mate and friend Gary Hamson said, 'Of all the players I played with and against, Woody was the greatest. I remember him scoring in one game, when we won 6-0. He picked the ball up in our half and when he hit it, he was still in the centre circle. When it left his boot, it looked like it was going out of the ground. It dipped at the last minute and smashed against the crossbar, and the entire ground – home and away fans – all stood and applauded. Woody had the hardest shot in football I've seen. His legs were like tree trunks.'

Chapter 14

UNITED HAD now won only once in five matches and were lurking perilously close to the bottom of the table. On 16 September, United finally won at home in the league – convincingly too. Gary Hamson scored twice, one from the spot, and Colin Franks and Mick Guy added to the joy to complete a much-needed 4-0 victory over Burnley.

Two days later, the Blades added some silverware to the trophy cabinet when they were victorious in the Sheffield and Hallam County Cup Final. The County Cup as it was known, was contested over the years by both Sheffield teams, as well as Rotherham, Barnsley and Doncaster Rovers. The Blades had won the first ever tournament held in the 1920/21 season, beating Wednesday 2-1 in the final.

The 1978/79 cup final was contested by Sheffield United and Doncaster Rovers. The venue was Bramall Lane. United gave a second start to new loanee keeper Nicky Johns, his debut having come in the Norton Woodseats game a week prior. The Blades fielded a strong side and Guy, Franks, Calvert and Stainrod all scored as they won 4-1. Haslam had brought in 20-year-old keeper Johns and Peter Anderson, on loan from

Florida side Tampa Bay Rowdies. Anderson had played under Haslam during his time in charge at Luton. He was on the bench for the trip to West Ham United on 23 September, as United were beaten 2-0.

Anderson's full debut coincidentally came against the Hatters at the end of September. He scored against his former club in the 1-1 draw.

Johns made his league debut in goal on 7 October against Sunderland. Despite United spending the last few years watching the pennies, the team that faced Sunderland had cost around half a million pounds, quite a princely sum by comparison.

An 18-year-old local lad, Richard Harwood, also made his debut. A mistake from debutant Johns gave Sunderland the lead. The noise inside Bramall Lane was deafening from the Sunderland fans chanting 'We're going to win the league!'

Anderson levelled in the second half after a run from Gary Hamson and a delightful diagonal pass – Anderson's second goal in two games. Sunderland then had a goal disallowed for offside. A chipped through-ball from Sabella found Anderson for his third goal in two games to silence the Sunderland fans. That goal was voted runner-up in *Match of the Day*'s goal of the season competition.

A solo run from Sabella took him past two defenders to get to the line, and pull the ball back for Finnieston to score an easy third for the Blades – his first for the club. Sunderland's substitute scored a consolation in injury time that was celebrated by the handful of Sunderland fans that remained in the ground.

United were 13th in October, as they faced Leeds United in the League Cup at Bramall Lane. There is always plenty of interest and anticipation when the Yorkshire rivals meet, but this one had a couple of extras. Tony Kenworthy was looking forward to showing the city in which he grew up what they had missed out on again, but the fans (and media) were more focused on the return of the great Tony Currie.

Yes, the fans now had an Argentinian superstar to worship, but he wasn't Tony Currie. As if to rub salt into the still open wounds of the Blades fans, Currie scored the opening goal in front of the Kop – in the wrong shirt.

Some fans remember a section of the Blades supporters chanting 'Currie is a fat twat'. John McNerney, a Blade for over 50 years, recalls Currie lifting his shirt and shrugging in response. Some were just happy to have seen Currie play one more time, while others claim to have erased it from their memory: simply too painful to remember.

Leeds led 0-2 at the interval and the game ended 1-4. After beating the best team in Europe in the previous round, the scoreline (and Currie scoring) was hard to take for United fans.

> On 12 October, former Sex Pistol Sid Vicious was arrested for the murder of his girlfriend, Nancy Spungen. Spungen was found in the couple's New York hotel room, with stab wounds to her stomach. Both Vicious and Spungen were heroin addicts, and the bassist denied her murder, claiming a drug dealer was responsible. Vicious would die of an overdose before he was brought to trial for the murder.

Steve Conroy replaced Johns in goal and saved a penalty as United drew away at Millwall, then beat Oldham Athletic 4-2 – Steve Finnieston, John Matthews, Gary Hamson and Simon Stainrod scored.

Sabella's sleek skills (on his left foot at least), while appreciated by Blades fans, were perhaps not best suited to England's Second Division and he had scored just once. He was a luxury that United couldn't afford, according to at least one ex-team-mate. His ability was undeniable, but his work rate could be questionable. Tony Kenworthy claimed in his autobiography *Blade Heart,* a couple of years ago, that Sabella refused to train on Fridays, as many foreign players did then. The second tier of English football was not the right place and 1978 was not the right time for Alex Sabella. Fans, though, gave him the benefit of the doubt and took him to their hearts. Despite the cold and the mud, and getting repeatedly kicked in every game, and beaten in most, Sabella kept his place in the side.

Anderson found the net again for United against Stoke City, but his goal wasn't enough as United lost 2-1. Imre Varadi, 19, was on the bench for the home defeat against Brighton on 4 November. He was on it again for the 1-1 draw away at Orient a week later, and again the following week in the 0-1 home defeat to Preston North End. Varadi came off the bench on the Tuesday night trip to Crystal Palace to score his first goal for the club, but the Blades lost 3-1.

Varadi's goal earned him a place in the starting line-up for the next game, away at Bristol Rovers on 25 November. Finnieston scored for United, but it was another defeat, Rovers winning 2-1. However, Varadi kept his place and scored his second for the Blades – away at Charlton Athletic – but once again it was nothing more than a consolation. The Addicks consigned United to their eighth game without victory.

By December, United had slipped to 19th place, having won just four times.

Colin Franks came back into the side, replacing John Cutbush against Cardiff City. Understandably crowds were starting to dwindle, and less than 12,000 fans were inside Bramall Lane to see the Blades finally win again. Anderson and Matthews scored in the 2-1 victory.

United won for a second consecutive league game for the first time since the previous December, on Boxing Day, at home to Newcastle United, Paul Garner scoring the only goal. At home to Cambridge United, Varadi scored twice, and John Matthews scored in a 3-3 draw in the last game of 1978.

Bobby Robson tried to sign United midfielder Mick Speight. Speight and his wife spent the weekend at the home of Sir Bobby and his wife Elsie. 'Two great people,' recalls Speight. 'We were shown around the club and the district, the house and everything. I must have made a good impression on the England tour. I was to replace Brian Talbot, who was being sold to Arsenal. I was happy with the offer. I thought the deal was done, until I received a call, saying the clubs couldn't agree a price. It just wasn't to be.'

The beginning of January brings the excitement of the FA Cup third round, and in January 1979 it brought Aldershot to Bramall Lane. Fourth Division Aldershot had lost their previous game to Wigan but had won ten of their 23 league games and were fifth in the division. Still, it was somewhat of an upset when they held United to a goalless draw. It was a bigger upset when they won 1-0 in the replay at the Recreation Ground.

On 10 January, Prime Minister James Callaghan returned to strike-hit Britain from a four-nation summit in Guadeloupe, to deny that the country was in crisis.

> His comments prompted the famous headline 'Crisis, what crisis?' Several strikes had taken place in protest at the government pay cap. A bakers' strike two months previous had resulted briefly in bread rations being introduced, to fend off panic buying.
>
> Opposition MPs called for a general election. Tory MP Michael Heseltine said, 'It's quite obvious Mr Callaghan is out of touch with the deteriorating situation in Britain ... to come back and suggest it all looks parochial is frankly patronising.' Those three words would come back to haunt Mr Callaghan, even though he never actually said them. They were the work of a *Sun* journalist.
>
> By the end of January, binmen, water workers, sewerage staff and emergency workers were all on strike. Green Goddesses, built in the 1950s and operated by military service men, were seen on the streets of England, deployed to cover for fire engines.

Harry Haslam responded to the defeat to lowly Aldershot by showing his shrewd business sense again, selling Imre Varadi to Everton for £80,000. Varadi had only played ten games for United, scoring four goals. He went on to play for over a dozen clubs including Newcastle United, where he scored 39 goals in 81 games, and he also played for the Blades' neighbours Wednesday in two separate stints. With the benefit of hindsight, what might have looked at the time like a good deal for the Blades, was possibly a terrible one.

Towering defender John MacPhail was signed from Dundee for £30,000 and Dougie Brown was recruited from Clydebank. Brown had started at Aberdeen, but failed to impress, and moved to Clydebank at the start of the season. He played 12 times for them, scoring once. MacPhail had signed for his hometown club, Dundee, at the age of 20. He was regarded as something of a legend by their fans. He made his Blades debut against Fulham in a 1-1 draw on 6 February. Another 1-1 draw followed, away at Luton Town, Gary Hamson equalising from the penalty spot.

The winter of 1978/79 – known as the winter of discontent, due to the strikes – was also the winter of extremely cold weather. Britain saw the heaviest snowfall in years as temperatures plummeted; and so did United.

The Blades failed to score in their next two games, conceding two at home to Millwall on a snowy pitch and four away at Wrexham, leaving United in 19th position.

Oldham Athletic were level with United on points, but a place lower on goal difference. The two sides shared the spoils in a 1-1 draw, a result that did little to help ease either side's relegation fears. Simon Stainrod, who had made a promising start to his United career, first partnering Keith Edwards before he was sold to Hull, was shipped out to Oldham for £60,000 to boost their survival chances. At the time, Stainrod was Oldham's record signing. He went on to score 21 goals for Oldham Athletic before moving to Queens Park Rangers, where he enjoyed his best spell, scoring 48 goals. During his time at QPR he played under Terry Venables. When Venables made the move to Barcelona, there was talk of him taking Stainrod with him to partner Steve Archibald, but the move never materialised. He, like former team-mate Varadi, also later had a spell at Wednesday.

Two further draws, away at Burnley and at home to Stoke City, saw United slip ever closer to the drop. Dougie Brown doubled his career goal count, scoring his first goal for United in a 4-1 defeat at Notts County and United then lost 2-0 at top-of-the-league Brighton, in a game that finished with both sides reduced to ten men.

Les Tibbott was bought from Ipswich Town for a fee rumoured to be around £100,000 and Bruce Rioch was brought in on a short-term loan from Derby County. Midfielder Rioch had enjoyed a successful career and despite being past his best by the time he joined United, was still a very capable player and brought some much-needed quality to the side.

Welshman Tibbott had come up through the Ipswich youth team, making his debut for Bobby Robson in 1976. He played 54 games for Ipswich, including an appearance in the FA Cup third round in the 1977/78 season. They won the trophy that year. He also won two under-21 international caps while at Portman Road.

Both men made their debuts at the end of March, in the home game with Bristol Rovers. Anderson scored the only goal of the game. Anderson scored twice in the next game, against West Ham United, Steve Finnieston scoring the other in a 3-0 victory.

United lost 2-0 at Blackburn Rovers the following week. On 10 April, at home to Notts County, who were now managed again by Jimmy Sirrel, John MacPhail scored his first goal. Captain Mick Speight scored twice, Alex Sabella grabbed one and Anderson completed the rout as United won 5-1 to the delight of their fans.

Rioch scored his first goal for the Blades against Newcastle United four days later in a 3-1 win to raise hopes of survival. Tony Kenworthy got a goal in the 1-1 draw with Wrexham at the Lane, but then Cardiff City put four past United without reply.

At Roker Park, after a close first half in which Kenworthy scored early on for United, Gary Hamson missed a penalty and United had three attempts cleared off the line. Alex Sabella scored a wonderful solo effort, but Sunderland thumped in four goals in the second period to stun the Blades 6-2, leaving United in the drop zone. Rioch's short loan ended and he returned to his parent club, Derby County.

Anderson and Guy scored as United beat Charlton Athletic 2-1 but defeats at Blackburn Rovers and then Cambridge United, meant that United needed to win the final game of the season at home to Leicester City, by three clear goals to survive. Leicester were two places and two points above United heading into the game and a three-goal margin could send Leicester down, depending on Oldham's result (a win, of course, was still only worth two points). Teenager Ian Benjamin made his full United debut, replacing Anderson.

The teams were level 1-1 at the break, with Benjamin scoring from the spot, leaving United 45 minutes to score three goals to stay in the division. Leicester had a man sent off and debutant Benjamin scored a second penalty, but the game ended 2-2 and United were relegated to the Third Division for the first time ever. The glory of beating Liverpool, who won the First Division title, was now a distant memory.

The Blades had spent just three seasons in Division Two, after so narrowly missing out on Europe two years before that. In five short, disastrous years Sheffield United had fallen from competing with the best teams in the country, with some of the most talented and exciting players in their ranks, to the lowest point in the club's history.

In that time, greats such as Len Badger, Ted Hemsley, Alan Woodward, Tony Currie, Billy Dearden and Keith Edwards had all been allowed to leave and had been replaced by inferior players. Defeat in the FA Cup to Aldershot paled into insignificance when compared to the humiliation of relegation to the third tier.

United fans were devastated and angry.

Unsightly scenes followed the Leicester game, with some fans running on to the pitch to vent their frustration at the opposition's players. As a result, Bramall Lane would have fences erected around the pitch.

In May, the Tories won the general election, by a majority of 43 seats, making Margaret Thatcher the first ever woman Prime Minister. Former Liberal leade, Jeremy Thorpe, awaiting trial at the time for conspiracy to murder, said he was horrified. Surely, things couldn't get any worse.

Chapter 15

THE CITY of Sheffield now had two Third Division teams.

Wednesday had been there for some time, having recently endured the worst period in their history, but had now engaged the services of former World Cup winner, Jack Charlton. They were bottom of the Third Division when Charlton replaced Len Ashurst at Hillsborough.

While United fans were still reeling from the hurt of relegation, Owls fans were much more optimistic and had raised expectations, particularly when Charlton controversially persuaded the talented Terry Curran to drop down two divisions to join his revolution from Southampton. The Owls had finished 14th in Division Three the previous season.

Chesterfield and Rotherham United, as well as Barnsley, who had just been promoted, were all in the third tier as well, so as the publication of the 1979/80 fixture lists approached, anticipation began to grow. Fans had not had local derbies to look forward to for years. Before the season began, United were also drawn against another local side, Fourth Division Doncaster Rovers, in the League Cup.

Gary Hamson was sold to Leeds for £140,000. In his first season at Elland Road, he played 19 First Division games under Jimmy Adamson. In October 1980, Adamson left, and Allan Clarke was put in charge. Clarke and Hamson didn't see eye to eye and Hamson found himself in the reserves. 'Clarke was a fantastic player, but as a person he was quite arrogant. I was angry. I learned early in my career that as a midfielder I was going to get kicked a lot. I used to make sure I got in first. I wasn't dirty but I'd make sure I looked after myself. I got sent off against Newcastle reserves – it was a stupid sending off, and I got a nine-match ban.'

Hamson was part of the Leeds team that were relegated from the First Division in 1982. He played 134 games for Leeds, scoring three times. In 1986, Hamson moved to Bristol City on a free transfer. Leeds could have received a fee, but then-manager Billy Bremner let his player move for free, so that Hamson could get some money out of the deal. At Bristol, Terry Cooper used to change his formation for away games and Hamson would only play in those games. At home the Robins played a formation that Hamson didn't fit, and he was left out. He made a dozen appearances for Bristol before moving to Port Vale for £10,000. Port Vale were bottom of the Third Division when Hamson arrived, despite having a decent team. Following his arrival, they went unbeaten for the rest of the season.

When the injuries and the operations caught up with him, a devastated Hamson was forced to retire from the game aged just 29. At 22, while still at Elland Road, Hamson had suffered a bad injury, damaging his cruciate ligament. A chain of unfortunate events followed. The Leeds doctor had cut his finger off in a gardening accident, so Hamson was forced to rely on the NHS. Unluckily for the young midfielder, the NHS were on strike. The operation, when it was finally carried out, was a disaster and further surgery was needed later.

He remained at Port Vale for a while as youth team coach. Businessman Billy Bell was chairman, having won control of the club after a bitter battle with Jim Lloyd. He was quoted as saying, at the time, 'There is no room for sentiment in football.' Bell had promised Hamson a pay rise when he gained his coaching badges, but when the team showed signs of improvement, Bell reneged on the agreement, saying he needed the money for players and ground improvements. A furious Gary Hamson walked away from the club and away from football. He remains good friends with many of the players he shared a dressing room with at Bramall Lane, and still attends games occasionally.

United signed Dutchman Len de Goey from Sparta Rotterdam for £125,000, and well-travelled striker Barry Butlin joined from Peterborough United. Butlin had started out at Derby County but after just a handful of games moved to Notts County on loan. He then moved to Luton, where he made 57 appearances, scoring 24 goals. In 1974 he moved to Nottingham Forest, where he scored 17 goals. During his time at Forest, he was part of the team that thrashed United 6-1. From Forest he moved to Peterborough for two years. He was 30 by the time he joined the Blades. He had scored 69 goals in 239 games.

Amid circulating rumours that Alex Sabella was wanted by Sunderland, United also signed a second Argentinian, sadly still not Maradona. Midfielder Pedro Verde signed from Hercules for about £35,000. Verde is the uncle of Juan Sebastian Veron, who played for some of the biggest clubs in world football, including Chelsea, Manchester United, Sampdoria and Lazio, and had started at Estudiantes. Veron's Uncle Pedro had played for slightly less illustrious teams. Like his nephew, Verde had started out at Estudiantes, before moving to Gran Canaria to play for Las Palmas and then Spanish side Hercules.

Defender Tony Moore also signed for the Blades from Northern Premier League (seventh tier) Worksop Town.

The warm-up to United's first ever season in the third tier began with a 1-0 win at home to Mansfield Town, with 4,875 witnessing Dougie Brown's winner on 31 July. Away at Cambridge United on 4 August, John Flood scored the winner in a second 1-0 victory. Three days later, Barry Butlin scored his first goal for United, at one of his former clubs, Notts County, in a third consecutive 1-0 victory.

On 9 August 1979, Brighton council announced it was to be the first major resort in Britain to dedicate one of its beaches to nudists. Councillor Eileen Jakes, a 47-year-old grandmother, led the campaign, believing the 200-yard section of the seafront would attract tourists. To help persuade her fellow councillors, she shared photographs of herself topless in Ibiza. The plan faced stiff opposition. One councillor called it a flagrant exhibition of mammary glands. The beach officially opened in April 1980.

For United, the serious business started on 11 August with the League Cup, when Doncaster Rovers came to Bramall Lane for the first of several local derbies that the fans were looking forward to. Moore and Tibbott both played at the back, Benjamin continued up front but missed a penalty and John Flood scored the United goal in the 1-1 draw. The replay three days later at Belle Vue saw De Goey make his debut and Trenton Wiggan named as a substitute. Dowd was sent off for Rovers but United still lost 1-3.

The league season opener at home to Swindon Town was attended by 12,020 fans. Cutbush returned to the side and young Ian Benjamin continued his run in the team from the end of the previous campaign. Swindon led at half-time but in a second-half revival, Benjamin equalised before Dougie Brown grabbed the winner.

An unchanged team went to Colchester on the Tuesday night, to lose 1-0. Cutbush was sent off in that game to compound the defeat. On the following Saturday away at Chester, Moore replaced the suspended Cutbush, and captain Mick Speight scored in the 1-1 draw. Won one, lost one, drawn one.

> Lord Mountbatten was killed on 27 August. The 79-year-old cousin of the Queen was on his boat, fishing, when an IRA bomb exploded, killing him and his grandson. Thomas McMahan was convicted of the murders after being arrested on suspicion of driving a stolen car a couple of hours before the explosion. He was released in 1998 under the Good Friday Agreement.

Following United's draw with Chester, unorthodox Haslam sprung another surprise on Blades fans by selling young striker Ian Benjamin to West Bromwich Albion for £125,000. Benjamin had made an immediate impact in the United side, scoring two on his league debut and one in his next league game. In total, he had played five games for United and scored three goals.

Ron Atkinson's West Brom had reached their highest league finish since 1953 the previous season, finishing third, in Atkinson's first season in charge. They also reached the quarter-final of the UEFA Cup. The influx of black footballers stole many of the headlines amid times of violence, hooliganism and racism. Cyrille Regis, Brendon Batson and Laurie Cunningham, nicknamed 'the Three Degrees' in the press, had taken the league by storm, but the brilliant Cunningham had left for Real Madrid at the end of the season, becoming the first ever English player to sign for the Spanish giants. Keen to not lose the momentum his side had gained, Big Ron moved players out and in.

One of the other players to leave the Hawthorns was Len Cantello. Cantello had been at the club for over a decade and at the end of the 1978/79 season, a special testimonial benefit match was held for him, in which a Cyrille Regis and Laurie Cunningham XI – a team made up entirely of black players – played against a white XI. The Regis Cunningham XI included Bob Hazel, Garth Crooks, Remi Moses, Derek Richardson, Brendon Batson and United's Ian Benjamin.

Baggies fan Andy Caulton wrote an article about the game for the Over the Bar website: 'There were dire warnings from the local council regarding this game, but simply look at the meeting of the captains for the traditional handshake. Len has his hand out to greet Cyrille. Cyrille's playful response, of his hand close to his face, making fun of Len says everything about the bond. I ADORE this gesture, and it's beautifully framed in time. It is perfect and sets the tone for what this game WAS about. Not what the media may have perceived it as ... Cyrille [RIP] nailed it. Got it perfectly right. Few people were as racially abused as he was as a player, and his gentle, generous, genuine response at the start of the game says everything about the occasion.'

Andy's full piece and many more great football articles can be found at Otbfootball.net

The story sounds unlikely today, and probably wouldn't be allowed now, but the event was well received and well played, without even a hint of the discrimination or racism that was so rife in the game at the time, even when the black team won 3-2 after Garth Crooks scored the winner.

Big Ron paid £100,000 to take Benjamin to West Brom. He played just twice for them before moving briefly to Notts County and then to Peterborough United. After 80 games and 14 goals for the Posh, Benjamin was signed by Northampton Town boss Graham Carr – TV comedian, Alan Carr's dad. In 1986/87 they won the Fourth Division title together. In 150 games for the Cobblers, he scored 58 goals. He finished his playing career at Wigan Athletic in 1996.

Meanwhile, Alex Sabella made his first start of the season on 1 September, at home against Exeter City, and opened the scoring. John MacPhail added a second, and John Matthews scored a penalty to make it 3-1. United then played Dundee in an Anglo-Scottish Cup qualifying match, and Dundee found their former defender MacPhail in magnificent form. Scotland manager Jock Stein was due to attend the game, but decided to wait for the St Mirren game in December. Tony Kenworthy says, 'John MacPhail was superb that night. He was a great mate of mine, and still is. On the field he was an animal, but he could play football as well. If Jock Stein had been at the Dundee game, MacPhail plays for Scotland.' United won 1-0, MacPhail scoring the winner.

Striker Jeff Bourne signed from Atlanta Chiefs. Bourne had started his career at Burton Albion, before spending six years at Derby. In 1976, Bourne went on loan to Dallas Tornado and after a season at Crystal Palace – where he scored nine in 15 games – he returned to Dallas. In his second spell in Dallas, he netted 21 times in 30 games before moving to Atlanta.

Bourne made his United debut in a 3-1 defeat at Hull City with Sabella again scoring for the Blades. United then went on something of a surge. Haslam's best run since taking charge at the club started with the first proper local derby of the season, against Barnsley. The Tykes had lost on the opening day at home to Wednesday, thumped 0-3, then had lost 2-0 to Chesterfield three days later. Two subsequent wins had settled them down, but not enough for them to be looking forward to a third local derby in a month. Bourne scored on his home debut to make it 1-0 to the Blades, before Matthews wrapped the game up with the second goal.

Back-to-back home games brought back-to-back wins, Blackpool this time on the receiving end, despite taking the lead. Tony Kenworthy scored his first goal of the season to equalise, before Bourne scored his second in two games. Mick Speight scored the third.

Bourne scored his third in as many games in a seven-goal thriller at Mansfield's Field Mill. Len de Goey and Barry Butlin scored their first league goals for United, Speight scored his second in two games and Bourne got the winner in a 3-4 victory. It was the first time United had won three consecutive league games since April 1977, when Keith Edwards had scored five times in three games.

Suddenly, there was some optimism among fans and over 17,000 were at the Lane for the visit of Oxford United. John

MacPhail made a superb save on the line after Conroy was beaten early on, and the resulting spot kick was dispatched to make it 0-1 to the visitors. Bourne scored yet again to level from the second penalty in the opening 20 minutes, after he was brought down in the box. De Goey was credited with the second for United, although it took a huge deflection, and Matthews scored the third to make it 3-1.

The result put United top of the league. Rotherham United were a point behind the Blades, in second place. Neighbours Wednesday were 12th in the table, having won just once at home.

The midweek trip to Blackpool on 3 October saw United's fifth win on the bounce. De Goey, MacPhail and Sabella all scored in the first half before a Blackpool comeback, but United doggedly hung on and clinched a 3-2 victory. Bourne and Butlin then scored a goal each at Millmoor to beat Rotherham 1-2 and extend the lead at the top.

A 2-1 loss at Colchester United was United's only defeat in what would turn out to be ten league games. Bourne scored twice in the last of those ten in a 2-1 win away at Brentford on 22 October. Neil Ramsbottom stepped in to replace Conroy in goal.

The Millers had slipped down the table, but Wednesday had shown improvements and sat one place below Rotherham in sixth position. United were seven points clear at the top of the league with Colchester United now their closest rival.

Bourne was on eight for the season so far and was in great form. Just short of 20,000 saw Millwall win 0-1 at the Lane. Tony Moore returned to the side that day, replacing Mick Speight.

The away game at St Mirren on 30 October in the Anglo-Scottish Cup finished goalless. It was the first time United had failed to score in consecutive games since the previous February. Another defeat on the road followed, this time at Swindon Town. United fought back from two down through MacPhail and Speight but still lost 3-2. A third consecutive defeat came at home to fourth-placed Brentford. The gap at the top was now cut to just one point.

John Cutbush came back into the side for the visit of Gillingham, after missing the previous seven games. Barry Butlin scored twice, Sabella got one and De Goey scored the fourth without reply.

Defeat at Carlisle United preceded the FA Cup first-round tie with minnows Burscough. It was only the second time the Cheshire County League side had qualified for the FA Cup, being beaten by Blyth Spartans in their previous attempt. The non-league outfit were originally drawn as the home team, but the tie was switched to Bramall Lane. Haslam, perhaps fearing the underdogs could provide a banana skin, but more probably not having enough depth in his squad, named an unchanged side. MacPhail, Speight and Matthews all scored as the Blades won 3-0 to shatter the non-leaguers' dreams for another year.

Remarkably, just 100 fewer fans than had attended the previous home game turned up for the cup tie. It was 100 more than came to Bramall Lane on 1 December for the next home game. Speight scored his third goal in a month, Sabella scored his fifth of the season and Bourne scored his first goal in eight games, as the Blades beat Plymouth Argyle 3-2.

Two days later, United headed north to face St Mirren in the Anglo-Scottish Cup again. The game was a catastrophe. Keeper Steve Conroy broke his arm during it, and the Blades were soundly beaten 4-0.

Neil Ramsbottom – whose former clubs included Wednesday – replaced the injured Conroy in goal as United travelled to Wimbledon. Butlin scored in the 1-1 draw.

United were drawn against Grimsby Town in the second round of the FA Cup. The Mariners were tenth in Division Three (United were still top, just). Ramsbottom remained in goal as United slipped out of the cup, losing 2-0. It would be Ramsbottom's second and final appearance for the Blades. Derek Richardson, the former Queens Park Rangers goalkeeper, replaced him for the next game, a friendly against Southend on 21 December. United won the game 2-0 but it was a peculiar time to hold the fixture, four days before Christmas, and even more strange considering who United's next opponents were.

On 26 December 1979, the two Sheffield clubs played each other in the league for the first time for nine years and it was the first time they had ever met in the third tier. It was the 100th meeting of the two teams. The build-up had been going on in the press and in the pubs for weeks. The media dubbed the game 'the South Yorkshire Cup Final'. Although the winter of discontent had been the previous year, there was still social unrest and public sector workers were still striking. Sheffield bus drivers decided to go on strike on Boxing Day, supposedly in protest at the threat of single crews and the proposed end of conductors on buses. The strike meant that fans would have to walk to the game in the freezing cold.

To add to the fun, Sheffield City Council, and the police, fearing trouble, brought the kick-off forward to 11am, before the pubs opened, with turnstiles opening at 9.30.

Over 500 police officers were inside the ground in one of the biggest police operations ever seen in Sheffield. Chief Supt

Peter Gratton – in charge on the day – described it as a military operation, saying they had been planning it since August.

There was so much razzmatazz laid on for the 50,000 (not including the police) inside Hillsborough, that the referee decided the teams should walk out of the tunnel side by side, like they do at Wembley cup finals. With such tension in the ground, it is little surprise that the hostilities spilled over before the players were even out on the pitch.

United skipper Mick Speight remembers the excitement, 'All week, it was all everyone was talking about. We were in good form and at the top of the table. We expected a good game with Wednesday, in front of a full house.'

Wednesday winger Terry Curran explained the importance of the game. Curran recalls watching local derby games as a kid in Hemsworth where he grew up. Even though there was often no more than 400 people there, he remembered the rivalry in those games – so says he knew what this game meant to the city. Curran had been a Wednesday supporter from the age of about 11, when he and his brother would play on the local park, and he would be Jim McCalliog.

He said, 'Kenworthy and MacPhail were at me in the tunnel, saying they were going to break my leg and I'd get carried off. I replied, "One: you're not technically good enough; and two: you're not fast enough to catch me … remember how you chased me round when you played Forest and we put six past you?"'

In truth, John MacPhail did tell Curran in the tunnel that he was going to do a number on him, but Kenworthy wasn't involved, and Curran didn't have a snappy reply, but he may have thought it.

The pitch at S6 was not in the best condition, following bad weather, and the mud did little to facilitate any quality football early on. Wednesday had an effort cleared off the line in the opening minutes. Ian Mellor opened the scoring for them with a shot from the edge of the area. United then pushed for an equaliser and hit the bar, Owls keeper Bob Bolder making a save from the rebound, which he knew little about. Wednesday led 1-0 at the break.

In the second half, Wednesday hit the post and bar in the same attack and Mick Speight's efforts to keep out the rebound resulted in him being carried off on a stretcher. 'To be honest, we didn't perform at all,' he recalls. 'I remember being carried off on a stretcher and taken to hospital. I had busted ribs and internal bleeding after a tackle in our box from a corner. They didn't score! I remember Cec [Coldwell] coming on and me telling him I couldn't breathe. He said, "Speighty, you have two lungs, use the other one." He strapped me up and stood me upright and I said "I'll see how it goes." From the next corner, I headed the ball away and just collapsed. That was me finished. I heard one of their players say, "That's it now – the game's ours."'

Whoever the Wednesday player was, he was correct. Speight's departure was the turning point in the game. Curran, the player who had dropped down two divisions to play for Jack Charlton, scored a diving header in front of the Blades fans. Soon after, Curran turned provider as his run ended in a third goal for Wednesday, this time scored by Jeff King (who later joined United). Derek Richardson then conceded a penalty, which was tucked away by Mark Smith to make it 4-0.

Jeff King marked Sabella out of the game, Tony Kenworthy explained: 'A lot of our players that Haslam had brought in weren't from Sheffield. They didn't understand what it meant, and they weren't up for it like some of us were. Sabella was a lovely bloke, but that wasn't his game. When you had to roll your sleeves up and go somewhere, he didn't want to know. Jeff King did a job on him, and Alex had no stomach for it.'

With such a scoreline, and a capacity crowd, trouble seemed inevitable, yet remarkably – amid such fierce rivalry – the police proudly reported after the game that not a single arrest was made inside the ground. The official attendance of 49,309 (which some say was on the conservative side) remains the biggest ever gate for a third-tier game.

The win saw Wednesday move up to fourth in the table; United were still top but the game meant much more than two points. It was not only a historic moment, one that the blue half of the city still refer to – far too often – every chance they get, even 40 years later, but a turning point. For years, Wednesday fans had lived with the knowledge their neighbours were doing so much better than they were. Now, they had something to celebrate, and they had momentum.

For United, it was a crushing blow. After years in the top flight, looking down on Wednesday, they had seen their best and most loved players sold. They had slipped from the verge of Europe to the Third Division, the lowest league they had ever been in, and now, the real dagger blow; they had lost bragging rights to their most bitter rivals, in what their fans dubbed 'the Boxing Day Massacre'.

Harry Haslam would need all his skill and charm to lift the players and the fans after the Boxing Day game. Fortunately, with it being the Christmas period, they would not have long to wait for the next game. Grimsby Town were the visitors to Bramall Lane on 29 December. The game ended in a 1-1 draw; Bourne scored for the hosts.

With the dawning of a new decade, there is often new hope. Pink Floyd's 'Another Brick in the Wall' was number one in the charts. Thatcher was still in power and the steelworkers went on strike. At British Steel Corporation plants across the country, they downed tools, demanding a 20 per cent pay rise, after management had offered them six per cent. British Steel employed 150,000 workers at the time, and it was thought around 90,000 walked out. The strike lasted almost 14 weeks before the union agreed a 16 per cent rise. Their success was short-lived though as later in the year 1,400 workers lost their jobs.

Sheffield United borrowed Viv Busby on loan from Stoke City. United hosted Blackburn Rovers on New Year's Day. Barry Butlin gave the Blades the lead in the first half and Les Tibbott scored in the second half in a much-needed 2-1 win. Chesterfield were 11th in the table, some 14 points behind the Blades and were United's next opponents. Viv Busby made his debut and scored in the second half, but the Spireites were two up by then.

Bourne scored a penalty, away at Exeter City on 12 January, and young Steve Charles made his debut but United were beaten, 3-1. Len De Goey scored in the 1-1 draw with Hull on 19 January. Busby's short cameo ended, and he headed to the States to play for Tulsa.

Butlin returned to lead the line against Mansfield Town, but it was defender John MacPhail that scored the winner. United then drew three of their next four, losing the other to Reading. Steve Charles scored his first Blades goal in that game. Charles was still a student when he signed for United at the start of January 1980. He had played for England schoolboys but then went to study at Columbia University in America. He returned to his home town to play for the Blades in midfield.

Two further draws – at home to Chester and away at Bury – saw Wednesday overtake United in the league table. The Owls were now second, while United occupied fourth place.

On 4 March, United scored nine goals. Pedro Verde scored two, Dougie Brown another two and De Goey, Charles, MacPhail and Smith all got one each as the Blades thrashed a select XI for Eddie Colquhoun's testimonial. World Cup-winning England goalkeeper, the great Gordon Banks, born in Sheffield, came on as a substitute for the guests, while 17-year-old Gary Brazil made his first appearance as a substitute for United.

Verde's two goals in the benefit match were enough for him to keep his place in the next fixture, and he celebrated with another goal in a 1-1 draw at Millwall. United were now sixth, with Chesterfield, Blackburn and Colchester separating the two Sheffield clubs.

Verde was on target again in the 1-0 win over Rotherham United before the Blades failed to score in their next two games. The goals had dried up and United were lacking in confidence as they lost 3-0 at Gillingham and drew 0-0 with Barnsley. Terry Poole was in goal at Oakwell – United's fourth keeper of the season.

The second testimonial in a month took place on 26 March. Two of United's favourite sons returned for the game to honour Micky Speight's ten years at the club. Tony Currie and Keith Edwards played in the 4-2 win, with Edwards scoring twice.

League form was terrible however, and United lost four of their next five, drawing the other. The other, incidentally, was the return match of the Boxing Day game against the Owls. As often happened in those days, United had been in action the day before – losing away at Southend United.

Before kick-off, Grimsby Town had opened up a three-point lead at the top of the table. Wednesday were second, with 50 points and a game in hand, as a result of a Terry Curran-inspired 14-match unbeaten run. United were sixth on 43 points but had played a game more than the Owls and won just once in their last ten games.

Over 46,000 were inside a sunny Bramall Lane – including Barry Davies and the *Match of the Day* cameras. Host Jimmy Hill pointed out as he introduced the action, that a couple of results could change the whole picture. Davis pointed out in his preliminary observations that very nearly 100,000 people would have seen the two Steel City derbies that year.

The outcome of the 101st Sheffield derby would hang largely on whether Tony Kenworthy could stifle Terry Curran. Kenworthy started alongside Cutbush, Tibbott and MacPhail, with Terry Poole in goal. The game promised to be a tasty affair, with MacPhail being fouled in the opening minute. Curran and Kenworthy tangled in the United box moments later, but referee Joe Worrall judged it six of one and half a dozen of the other, and waved play on.

Wednesday had the better of the opening exchanges and Mellor produced a good save from Poole. It was a scrappy game, lacking in any real quality or poise, but Sabella showed moments of class, finding time to dwell on the ball whenever possible. One surging run from the little Argentinian almost created a chance for Speight but his shot whistled wide of the post.

After another tussle between Kenworthy and Curran, when the referee gave Curran a free kick, the Wednesday man slapped Kenworthy on the cheek, trying to prompt a reaction. Kenworthy reacted angrily – shoving Curran away. As the referee called both players over, the Wednesday man proceeded to step on Kenworthy's foot. Remarkably the referee seemed to miss it, despite being only a yard away and looking straight at them.

Kenworthy, who was by no means a softie, writhed on the ground in pain as boos and chants rang around the ground. After Cec Coldwell had run on to the pitch to treat Kenworthy, the defender was able to continue, to what appeared to be sarcastic applause from Curran.

It was another defender that scored the opening goal, John MacPhail tapping in a rebound off the post from a Sabella free kick, which was looped up by Butlin, to make it 1-0 just before half-time. Curran, apart from his underhand tactics, had had little impact on the game so far and it was Kenworthy that seemed in control.

The half ended with the United fans in full voice and 'Hark now here!' echoing around the stands.

United started the second half brightly with Speight testing the Owls keeper, Bolder, early on. As the half progressed though, Wednesday began to enjoy some possession and started to press. They were awarded a seemingly harmless throw-in near the corner flag. Curran received the ball wide, surrounded by three players. He danced past the three of them until he was on the edge of United's area before unleashing a terrific shot past Terry Poole.

Alan Biggs, a local sport journalist for over 50 years, describes the goal as the best he has ever seen live, to this day.

It was undoubtedly a fabulous goal, but to be fair, the United players surrounding him – one of whom was Sabella – failed to put in a challenge between them. Barry Davies said of Curran, 'He's a character – and when he wants to, he can play.'

Unfortunately for the Blades, it seemed when Curran faced them, he wanted to play. Kenworthy was suffering with an injury and the game continued as he sat on the floor. Play eventually stopped so he could be treated, but he was unable to continue and had to be carried from the pitch. Forward John Flood came on to replace him, and young Phil Jones dropped in to mark Curran. Jones had made his debut for the reserves as a 15-year-old but found appearances in the first team limited.

The game finished level and afterwards, Barry Davies interviewed both managers. Haslam claimed that despite Wednesday taking three out of four points from his side this season, there were still plenty more games to go, with United still with some top sides to play.

Refuting Barry Davies's comment which suggested he didn't always want to play, Owls goal-scorer Curran says, 'I wanted to beat every team I played against.' He adds, 'The game wasn't as good as the Boxing Day game, but I scored a great goal. Not just a great goal for me but an important goal. It saved a point and kept up our promotion chase … as well as stopping United beating us.'

As Haslam had said, there were plenty more games to play; indeed, the next game was just two days later, their third in four days, away at promotion-chasing Blackburn Rovers. United lost 1-0. Mid-table Plymouth Argyle were United's next opponents and thrashed them 4-1. The Blades would only win one of their last five matches and finished the season in a disappointing 12th place. Rotherham United, themselves promotion contenders earlier in the season, finished a place behind United.

Grimsby Town's 4-0 demolition of United on the final day clinched the title for them. Blackburn went up and Wednesday were also promoted, giving their fans yet more bragging rights and United fans more reason to be disappointed.

After being given a testimonial towards the end of the season, captain Mick Speight was sold to the newly promoted Blackburn Rovers for around £60,000. Speight had made 199 first team appearances for the Blades over ten years, playing in three different divisions and scoring 14 goals. As a senior member of the team, and now club captain, he had the ear of both manager and coach.

He says, 'I was as surprised as anyone when I heard Howard Kendall was interested in me. I had a great relationship with Harry Haslam and Danny [Bergara]. We'd been discussing the type of player we needed to bring in to get us going back up the leagues quickly. We needed a strong striker with experience. That striker would be Bob Hatton. We had just finished a pre-season run and I was heading back to the training ground, when out of the blue came big Bob. I was smiling from ear to ear and thought yes! Here we go. A couple of minutes later, I was called in to the office and to my surprise, told that the club had received an offer from Blackburn Rovers, who had just won promotion to Division Two. I was taken aback but was informed that the club had granted me permission to talk to them. After a lengthy discussion with Harry and Danny, I realised the club had more of a wish to sign Bob than to keep me, and I was the one player they could get money for.

'I needed time to think – and think hard. United had been my only club, and the one that had given me the chance to eventually captain the team, at all levels within the club, and got me international recognition. I had always thought – and hoped – that I would eventually be a coach and even a manager after I finished playing. I spoke to Howard and Mick Heaton – a friend and a former Blade. They sold Blackburn Rovers FC to me, and I eventually signed.

'Blackburn as a club were very much like Sheffield United – a family. They made it really easy for me to settle in. We had a great season and just missed out on promotion in the very last game of the season. I was voted player of the year. The next season, I was injured and missed most of the season with a ruptured thigh muscle that almost ended my career.'

After making 51 appearances for Blackburn, Speight moved again in 1982. 'I moved to Grimsby Town, another great family club. They were a very good side and I enjoyed playing there. In my second season with them, I picked up another thigh injury, which cost me a full season on the sidelines.

'I now had to think very hard where I wanted to go as a player-coach, and eventually manager – that was my aim. I had three offers and finally chose Chester City, under John McGrath, as player-coach. I learned so much from him. John became very ill and had to step down from the manager's position, and I was asked to take over. At the time, we were bottom of Division Four, and struggling. I said yes and set about getting us back on track.

'Chester was a place for learning survival, how to work with nothing – building and selling to survive. Thanks to picking up some good young players and developing the very good ones, it was a great challenge. I brought a younger striker in on loan from Everton, called Stuart Rimmer, who went on to be sold to Watford for a good sum – over £200,00. I picked up a young right-back, given a free transfer from Burnley. He went on to be a very classy player for both Arsenal and England: Lee Dixon.

'One local player was Andy Holden, a centre-back that went on to play for Everton and Wales. We had a good mixture of young lads and established players.'

Speight continues: 'We were bottom when I took over and our only goal was to not be relegated. Thankfully, with great effort and very good staff around me, we did it. I was promised the role permanently if we stayed up. We turned up for pre-season to find another manager had been brought in. The chairman brought in his old mate.

'I was heartbroken, and very annoyed. They asked me to stay on in my capacity as player-coach, which I did, but after that kick in the balls, I found it hard to motivate myself, particularly after being lied to. I played until November, then made the choice to leave. It was a hard choice, but when you're not enjoying your work, that you have given over 20 years to, you have to stand up and be counted. My time at Chester City helped me on my way to coaching and management, and what a journey it turned out to be.'

During his 26 years as a player, Mick Speight played with and against some of the finest players in the country, and even took that a step further, when he was called up to the England B team in 1978. He also played for some of the best coaches and managers.

'Having had many different coaches, and learning from all of them, you pick out the bits that suit yourself and your beliefs in how you wish to teach, develop and see the game. From my early years, I don't think we were ever really coached. By that,

I mean I had to do things in a certain way, or I was allowed to be myself, analyse myself, look for weak points and correct them. Coaches encouraged us to think outside the box. This allows you to develop and as the old saying goes, play off the cuff; playing blind, seeing it before it happens. Your football intelligence just increased. Playing with top players, and listening to them, they were the best coaches ever! Learning-by-doing is a great saying.

'Learning your role in the team is also really important. It's a team game, filled with individuals. Each player has his own identity, and these skills must be put into a complementary framework. Learning from the start, how to build a team was an important aspect of being a good player-coach. The captain's role is also an area that is very creative. Here you develop your leadership skills, and ability to take care of people – both on and off the field. As captain, you are the boss's right-hand man. There's a very strong bond when you're played as captain. The way of bringing out the best in other people, even when things are not going well, is a great leadership quality. The off-field club ambassador is also a very privileged role. You are always being watched and assessed by all around you. You represent your club 24 hours a day, seven days a week. It's a tough life but a fantastic one. The honour of being club captain is so high for any player. I was lucky enough to be given that great position at all my clubs. I just loved it! I embraced it and was thankful for the opportunity.'

Of two of the great coaches that Mick Speight played under, Danny Bergara and Howard Kendall, he says, 'Danny was a great tactician – he brought to the team great information. Every single player improved technically. I loved Danny. His thoughts and his way of playing were modern and always attack-minded. He was always two to three moves in front of the rest. He knew all the opposition's weaknesses and exposed them. His training was always fun and creative, but serious. A great friend, coach and gentleman.

'Howard was just a great player and motivator; he could build a side and get the best out of every player.'

Following his departure from Chester, Speight moved to Norway, where he managed a number of clubs. He still lives there today.

The long-anticipated sale of Alex Sabella was confirmed, and the talented Argentinian headed to Leeds United in a deal worth £400,000. He never really achieved his potential at Bramall Lane or at Elland Road. He was certainly a gifted player, but he was just in the wrong place at the wrong time. If he and former coach Bergara were around today, they would set the league on fire.

In spite of this, Sabella is warmly remembered by fans of both clubs, and when he managed the Argentina national team at the 2014 World Cup, he was reclaimed by supporters in Sheffield, as a Blade. Once a Blade, always a Blade.

Even today, when asked about Sabella, fans talk of his skill and brilliance over his inability to tackle or his one-footedness. He played 23 games for Leeds United, scoring twice before moving on again, back to his native Argentina. In his half a season at Elland Road, he helped Leeds finish ninth in the First Division.

While Sabella was manager of Estudiantes, before becoming the national coach, John Helm, who was covering the 2009 Copa Libertadores, and had, of course, first met the Argentinian in 1978, had dinner with him. Helm recalls Sabella expressing his gratitude to Sheffield United and saying that he believed his move to Bramall Lane was the making of him. At the time Haslam discovered him, he stood little chance of getting in the international side, as the likes of Mario Kempes and Osvaldo Ardiles were his competition, and they were ahead of him, but the move to United gave him great media exposure. It also gave him an opportunity, as a young man, to experience different cultures and different ways to play the game – experiences that would benefit him later as a coach.

On 25 November 2020, Sabella was admitted to hospital with fluid in his legs and was later moved to intensive care. He died on 8 December of heart disease. His death came just two weeks after that of the man that nearly took his shirt at United, fellow countryman Diego Maradona.

The club posted a message on Twitter saying, 'Sheffield United are deeply saddened to hear of the passing of former player Alejandro Sabella. Rest in peace Alex.' Just as Sabella had expressed his gratitude to United, Blades fans repaid that gratitude. They took to social media in their thousands to pay their respects. Although he only played 23 games for Leeds, their fans remembered him warmly too.

Argentina legend Lionel Messi thanked his former manager for helping create some of his greatest memories. Messi wrote on his Instagram account: 'It was a pleasure to share so much with you. Alejandro was a great person, aside from being an impressive professional who shaped my career, and I learned a lot from him. We experienced some of my best memories in football together during the World Cup qualifying stage and also at the World Cup. My condolences to all his family and friends.'

Liverpool retained the 1979/80 First Division title, finishing two points ahead of Manchester United, who enjoyed their highest league finish in ten years. Leicester City, who narrowly avoided relegation the previous season were Second Division champions, finishing a point above Sunderland.

Grimsby Town achieved their second promotion in two years, winning the Third Division title, ahead of Blackburn Rovers and Wednesday. Huddersfield Town and Walsall were promoted from the Fourth Division and would face the Blades in Division Three in season 1980/81.

Chapter 16

UNITED BROUGHT in young midfielder Mike Trusson from fellow Third Division side Plymouth Argyle and striker Bob Hatton from Luton Town. United were 32-year-old Hatton's eighth club.

Born in Hull, journeyman Hatton started his career at Wolves but after only ten games he moved to Bolton Wanderers, where he scored just two goals in 24 games. After a year at Bolton, he spent 12 months at Northampton Town, before spending two years at Carlisle United. In 1971, he moved to Freddy Goodwin's Birmingham City for £80,000.

He scored 58 times in 175 games for Birmingham in a forward line that included Trevor Francis and Bob Latchford, but it was at Blackpool that he enjoyed his most prolific spell. After joining the Seasiders for £60,000 Hatton scored twice on his debut in a 4-1 win. He made 75 appearances for Blackpool scoring 30 goals before moving again, this time to Luton Town.

In two years at Luton, he scored 29 goals before United identified him as the right candidate and Harry Haslam paid £100,000 to bring him to the Lane and persuaded him to drop down a division.

The Blades also bolstered their defence, bringing in experienced left-back Stewart Houston on a free transfer. The Scot had played 250 games for Manchester United and had helped them to the Division Two title in 1975 as well as being part of the team that reached the FA Cup Final in '76, although he didn't play in the showpiece. He was capped by Scotland in 1975.

Houston was also joined at Bramall Lane by former World Cup hero, Martin Peters, who had famously scored the second goal in England's World Cup Final glory. He had played over 300 games for West Ham United and over 180 for Tottenham.

When Peters joined Spurs, his £200,000 price tag was a British record. In 1975 Peters joined Norwich City. He was voted their player of the year two seasons in a row and scored 44 goals during his time there.

Although now 35, and well past his prime, Haslam signed Peters with the intention of grooming him to be the next manager. An insignificant fee was paid to the Canaries to bring him in as player-coach.

Peters was never a prolific goalscorer but brought some great pedigree to Bramall Lane, that Haslam thought would help United get out of the Third Division.

Preparations for the 1980/81 season began with another participation in the Anglo-Scottish Cup. Derek Richardson kept the keeper's jersey, and Stewart Houston made his debut alongside John Cutbush, Les Tibbott and John MacPhail. Mike Trusson started in midfield alongside Trenton Wiggan. Bob Hatton made his debut up front.

Trenton Wiggan had been a product of the youth academy after moving from Jamaica as a child. He had been just 16 when he made his first-team debut as a substitute the previous season, in the League Cup defeat to Doncaster Rovers, before he had even signed a professional contract.

Now he was given his first start, away at Chesterfield. United lost 1-0.

The second game of the tournament saw Peters, Hatton, Trusson and Houston all make their home debuts against Hull City. Tony Kenworthy made his first start of the season. Hatton scored twice as the Blades beat the Tigers 2-1. Steve Charles came into the team for the third game, away at Grimsby Town. United lost 1-0 and exited the tournament.

Newly promoted Wednesday were the next opponents in the first round of the League Cup. It was a much more low-key affair than the two league meetings the previous season, and just under 24,000 were at Hillsborough to see the Owls run out 2-0 winners. The second leg three days later finished 1-1, Hatton scoring for the Blades, but the bragging rights once again went to S6.

While Wednesday made their first appearance back in the Second Division at home to Newcastle United, the Blades travelled in the other direction, to Carlisle United's Brunton Park for their first league game of the season. Trenton Wiggan, after playing all the pre-season games, was left out. Steve Charles also dropped out, with Barry Butlin coming in. Bob Hatton scored two on his league debut and Martin Peters scored on his, as the Blades won 3-0.

Peters scored again in the next league game, at home to Chesterfield. Butlin also scored, as United ran out 2-0 winners. The Blades made it three wins out of three at home to Oxford United, as Bob Hatton scored the game's only goal.

It had been nine years since the Blades last boasted a 100 per cent record after three games, back in 1971/72, when they had finished tenth in Division One. That season, Sheffield United had gone ten unbeaten at the start of the campaign, and fans hoped they would see a similar run this season – and win promotion back to the Second Division, along with their annoying neighbours.

On 30 August, United travelled to Oakwell to play a decent Barnsley side that included defender Mick McCarthy and Ronnie Glavin. Barry Butlin put United in front after Houston found Hatton in space on the left. Barnsley levelled just before half-time. Barnsley striker Derek Parker celebrated by jumping around and, as Tony Kenworthy puts it, 'Getting in my face. So, I decided I was going to clatter him first chance I got. I did, and I enjoyed it. He deserved it. At half-time Martin Peters came raging into the dressing room and said he never wanted to see one of his players stamp on an opponent. Peters was playing in midfield, and he'd missed every tackle he'd gone in for. I said, "For starters, it wasn't a stamp, and secondly, I'm not your effing player. You go out there and try putting in an effing challenge."'

Peters was already trying to assert himself with the players. He may have not liked Kenworthy's style; he was used to slick passing from quality players and clean tackles from polished First Division defenders, although defenders in those days could put it about even in the First Division.

Like Alex Sabella had struggled to adapt to the English lower leagues, Peters certainly found Third Division life difficult. The game was very different to the level he had played at, and he himself was not in his prime.

Barnsley came back to win 2-1.

At home to Swindon Town at the start of September, Mike Trusson hit a post and Bob Hatton rattled the crossbar. Later,

Les Tibbott was brought down by the Swindon keeper, giving the referee no option but to award a penalty. Tony Kenworthy comfortably converted from the spot, slotting the ball into the keeper's left-hand corner. Kenworthy's goal separated the two teams at half-time.

In the second half, United missed a string of chances, then eventually, from a corner in the 78th minute, Peters, arriving at the back post, stooped to score the second.

Less than five minutes later a mis-aimed volley from John Matthews found Trusson in space to score his first for the club. Cries of 'We're going to win the league' echoed around the ground.

Trusson had been spotted by Plymouth Argyle while playing local amateur football at the age of 14. He signed for the under-15s side and made his first-team debut at 17, before turning professional at 18. Despite Argyle being relegated from the Second Division that season, Trusson stayed and made 80 appearances, scoring 19 goals.

The 19th of those goals was against United, in the previous season's 4-1 defeat for the Blades.

His first goal for United wrapped up the 3-0 win, putting the Blades top of the league. After the game, Haslam reiterated his belief that Martin Peters was there to quietly learn the ropes before taking over from him. Peters himself seconded Haslam's thoughts, saying it would be a slow process that would hopefully carry on for a couple of years. 'We're not going to take things too quickly – one step at a time. If we feel the time is right for me to take over, we'll do it when we want to.'

Haslam quipped in typical Haslam style, 'They've got Peters and Lee, now we've got Peters and me.'

On 6 September, Sheffield Wednesday visited Oldham Athletic. Owls hero Terry Curran would come up against former United striker Simon Stainrod, now an Oldham Athletic player. With Oldham leading 2-0 the ball went out for a throw-in, and Stainrod allegedly punched Curran in the chest. The Owls man responded by raising his knee and aiming it at Stainrod's groin. Although Curran says his knee failed to make contact, Stainrod fell to the floor and Curran was shown a red card, enraging the travelling Wednesday fans. Following the incident there were disturbances and players and managers tried to calm the crowd as lumps of concrete were pulled from the crumbling terrace and used as missiles.

Owls boss Jack Charlton was so disturbed by the scenes that he was reportedly close to tears. Although not quite a riot, the unpleasant incident was shown on ITV's *Calendar* programme, and pictures appeared in the national press. As a result of the incident Wednesday fans were banned from standing at games.

A week later, United were beaten 1-0 at Reading, but on the Tuesday night they thrashed Blackpool 4-2 at Bramall Lane. Tony Kenworthy opened the scoring for United from the penalty spot, his second penalty conversion in ten days, confidently sending the Blackpool keeper the wrong way. Barry Butlin scored the second and Steve Charles and Bob Hatton put the game beyond doubt.

United then lost three consecutive games, away at Huddersfield Town, at home to Rotherham and away at Blackpool. Trenton Wiggan scored his first senior goal for the Blades in the defeat at Bloomfield Road.

United brought in defender John Ryan who, like many of the personnel now at Bramall Lane, had played previously for Luton Town. Ryan scored on his debut, in the defeat to Rotherham, with a long-range pile-driver.

> Prime Minister Margaret Thatcher made a defiant speech in October, in response to growing calls for her to change economic policy. 'For those waiting with bated breath for that favourite media catchphrase, the U-turn, I have one thing to say. You turn if you want to, the lady's not for turning,' she said to rapturous applause from her Tory colleagues.

On 4 October, United drew 0-0 with Plymouth Argyle and following that, the Blades failed to win the next two games. Trusson and Jones scored in a 3-2 defeat to Burnley and Charlton Athletic beat United 2-0.

The shocking sequence of results – two wins in ten games – had seen United quickly drop to 15th in Division Three. Chesterfield now topped the table, with Rotherham United in fifth.

United met Newport County, who were two places below them. Mike Trusson scored his third of the season and Bob Hatton netted his fifth, as United won 2-0. Their next opponents, Exeter City, were beaten 3-1 with goals from Steve Charles, Martin Peters and Bob Hatton.

Haslam then paid around £70,000 to Exeter for their winger Steve Neville. Neville had started as an apprentice at Southampton under Lawrie McMenemy, where he made a handful of appearances. He was part of the Saints team, captained by Alan Ball, that was promoted from Division Two, before he moved to Exeter in 1978 for £15,000 where he had hit 22 goals in his 93 league games.

Neville made his Blades debut against Millwall the following week. United won for a third consecutive time again, beating the Lions 4-1 at the Den and Neville had a debut to remember, scoring United's third goal and being credited in some papers with the fourth, moving United back up to eighth in the table.

Trusson and Charles were both on target as United drew 2-2 away at Gillingham, then, at home to Colchester United on 1 November, Tony Kenworthy dispatched his third penalty of the season to open the scoring in the first minute, before Trusson and Charles made it 3-0, for United's seventh win out of nine at home.

United then drew two and lost two: 0-0 with Burnley, 3-2 away at Chester, 1-0 at Chesterfield and 2-2 at home to Carlisle United. In that match, the Blades twice came from behind and Tony Kenworthy scored both goals, including another penalty, his fourth of the season.

On the evening of Monday, 17 November, after four games without a win, United faced an all-star XI made up from some of the United side that were promoted to the First Division in 1970/71 (and guests), in a benefit match for former Blades defender John Flynn.

Flynn had been at Bramall Lane since 1969 and by 1971 had cemented his place in the defence alongside Eddie Colquhoun, under John Harris. He made 23 appearances in the Blades' first season back in the top flight, scoring three goals. He remained a regular in the side, until being given a free transfer to Rotherham in 1978. His benefit match was attended by just over 3,000 fans.

There were some unlikely names on the team sheets, including Norman Hunter, Billy Bremner, Alan Ball and even one Terry Curran. Curran was still a regular for Wednesday at that point, and really deserves some praise for simply having the balls to accept the invitation. Despite being booed by Blades fans – in true pantomime fashion – every time he got the ball, he didn't hide away and scored two goals in a celebration that finished 8-4.

Curran showed even more balls a few years later, when he signed for United. Another story for another book.

The next game was in the FA Cup first round. Stockport County held the Blades to a goalless draw. In the replay three days later the game again finished level, 2-2 this time, with goals from Charles and an own goal to send the match into extra time. Tony Kenworthy was the United hero again, scoring the winner early in overtime.

Walsall were United's next opponents. The 2-2 draw with Carlisle United had left the Blades in ninth place, the Saddlers were in 14th. Peters, still not finding it easy at this level, pulled out and was replaced by Barry Butlin, whose goal was the difference at half-time. Tony Kenworthy added a second goal early in the second half, again from the penalty spot. United looked to be strolling but somehow Walsall clawed their way back into the game at 3-3.

When Bob Hatton scored his second of the game in the last minute, the travelling Blades fans thought they had won it. Some of them remember frolicking on the ground, slightly the worse for wear, rolling in the snow that had fallen. By the time they had stood back up – wet and cold – the scores were level again, as Walsall responded immediately with an injury-time equaliser to make it 4-4.

It was a game that United could and should have won. Little did anyone know then, that dropping a point, taking one, rather than two, would have such utterly devastating consequences later.

Mike Trusson scored the solitary goal that beat Portsmouth at Bramall Lane in the first game of December. Two days later, on Monday, 8 December, the Blades beat Doncaster Rovers 4-2 in the County Cup Tony Kenworthy scored the first goal, from 12 yards.

> That was the day that John Lennon was shot dead. The 40-year-old ex-Beatle was gunned down as he entered his Manhattan apartment. Mark Chapman was charged with Lennon's murder. He claimed to have heard voices in his head, telling him to shoot the singer, just hours after Lennon had signed a copy of *Double Fantasy* for him. Chapman waited outside Lennon's home until the singer returned, then shot him four times. In the weeks following his death, 'Just Like Starting Over' and *Double Fantasy* topped the charts as well as three other singles featuring highly in the Top 10. Chapman remains behind bars, having had his parole denied 11 times.

Bob Hatton scored in a 1-1 draw in the FA Cup second-round match against Chesterfield, a game blighted by bad weather and a swirling wind. The weather had improved little for the replay three days later, nor had United's form: Chesterfield won 1-0.

Against Hull City on 20 December, Bob Hatton opened the scoring, after leaving a defender on his backside and poking the ball into the net from the edge of the area. Later, Conroy in goal gathered the ball and launched it long to Steve Neville, who ran at the Hull defence before finding

Hatton unmarked, to thump home his second of the game. Les Tibbott was credited with the third goal, but in truth it took a huge deflection that wrong-footed the Hull keeper. The game finished 3-1 to the Blades. The scorer for Hull was Keith Edwards from the spot, in front of the Kop.

United were eighth at Christmas, 1980. Charlton Athletic were runaway leaders at the top of the league and Hull City were bottom of it. The gap between the Blades and the promotion places was still relatively small: small enough for United fans to still hold out hopes of a promotion surge in the second half of the season.

On Boxing Day, Bob Hatton scored for United as the Blades lost 1-2 at Craven Cottage. The final game of 1980 was a 0-0 draw with Brentford, attended by 13,130.

The new year got underway at mid-table Newport County; the Welsh team won 4-0. The next match saw United slip to a 1-0 defeat at Portsmouth.

Manager Harry Haslam, who had been ill for a while, was absent for the game against Gillingham on 17 January and Martin Peters took charge for the first time. Gary Brazil was named as a substitute for the first time, while Tony Kenworthy was absent from Peters' first team sheet. The Blades lost 0-1, in front of just 8,778 fans.

United had lost the opening three games of the new year without finding the net. It was the final straw for the ailing Haslam, and he resigned the following day, leaving Martin Peters in the hot seat, sooner than he or anyone else anticipated.

Although in ill health, Harry Haslam wasn't quite finished in football. He was part of Bobby Robson's England set-up as they prepared for the 1982 World Cup in Spain. He continued to act as a scout until his death in 1986. Harry Haslam might not have brought success to Sheffield United, but he did bring some excitement and a little Argentinian to the city, and is fondly remembered by people in the game.

Martin Peters' first game as manager of Sheffield United ended in a 2-0 defeat away at Oxford United, the Blades' fourth game without a goal. His first home game in charge was against Reading. A first-half goal from Bob Hatton ended the drought and gave United the lead, and Steve Neville scored a second to give Peters his first win.

Peters had undoubtedly enjoyed a brilliant career as a player, but as a manager he had little respect from the dressing room or for the dressing room and rarely entered into dialogue with his players, not even his skipper Kenworthy. The former World Cup winner was never comfortable with his colleagues, and players and members of the press found him aloof.

One seasoned journalist remembers being at a dinner at Elland Road, where the survivors from the World Cup-winning team were all invited. All that were well enough to attend did, except for Peters, who after promising all week that he would attend, sent his apologies at the last minute.

At United, he continued to pick himself to play occasionally and started the game at Swindon Town on 14 February. Derek Richardson returned in goal for the trip to Wiltshire and young forward Trenton Wiggan got another run-out. United were three down by the break. The ever-reliable Kenworthy converted a second-half penalty and Hatton added a second, but the game finished 5-2.

Kenworthy was dropped for the following game with promotion hopefuls Rotherham United, widening the rift between the manager (who again picked himself) and the defender still further. Mike Trusson gave the Blades a first-half lead but two second-half goals for the Millers sealed another defeat for Peters.

United were now 13th in the table. Rotherham United had narrowed the gap at the top and were quickly catching leaders Charlton Athletic. Promotion now seemed a long shot for the Blades and there was some concern among fans, even though there was no immediate cause for worry, as they were well above the relegation zone in February.

Huddersfield Town sat fourth in the table but came to the Lane on the back of two defeats to Swindon Town and Reading. Snow had fallen before the game and it had to be cleared from parts of the pitch, so that the markings could be seen. The rest of the surface was little more than mud and sand.

Bob Hatton put United ahead from inside the box with just over ten minutes gone. Wiggan, described by one fan as a speedboat without a rudder, used his pace and strength to outrun and out-muscle two defenders before squaring to the unmarked Hatton.

A corner swung in by John Ryan met the head of the unmarked Wiggan for goal number two, but the game finished 2-2.

There was already talk of manager Peters regretting taking charge, and some reports said he was close to quitting, having only won once since he took over. The next game was at home to top-of-the-league Charlton Athletic. Peters brought in experienced striker Don Givens.

As a teenager Givens had been a prolific goalscorer for Dublin Rangers. He started his professional career at Matt Busby's Manchester United in 1965 but did not play a game until 1969, when he scored on his debut against Shamrock

Rovers. After just eight games for the Red Devils, he moved to Birmingham City. He played 59 games for them, scoring ten goals before going on loan to Bournemouth, where he scored four goals in five games.

He had won over 50 caps for the Republic of Ireland, and played in the European Championship qualifiers for them in 1980, although they were eliminated in the early stages after winning just twice and finishing third.

Givens made his United debut against the Addicks. Hatton smashed in a great opener for the Blades inside the first five minutes, giving the keeper no chance, after a flick-on from debutant Givens. Another Givens flick-header saw Hatton hit the post and left-back Paul Garner followed up to put away the rebound.

Wiggan used his strength to beat a defender and feed Givens, who fired home a third for the Blades, with the match commentator claiming 'the United followers hail a new hero'.

The 3-2 win against the league leaders left the Blades 14th in the table with ten games left to play. Ian Porterfield's Rotherham United were second in the table, chasing Charlton Athletic, and Portsmouth and Huddersfield Town were close behind the Millers. At the other end, Hull City, who had occupied bottom spot for most of the season, were still there.

Swindon Town were 18th and all of the teams below them were in danger of being sucked into a relegation battle. United had the luxury of a three-point cushion above the group.

United's next game was a trip to tenth-placed Exeter City. It was 0-0 at the break, but both sides scored in the second half, Tony Kellow for City and Steve Charles on target for United to earn another point.

On 26 March, four centrist Labour party defectors – known as 'the gang of four' – forged a new party, promising to heal divisions between the classes. Roy Jenkins, David Owen, Bill Rodgers and Shirley Williams founded the Social Democratic Party (SDP). They said their new party would campaign for environmentally friendly policies, equal opportunities for women and for ethnic minorities, and a fairer distribution of wealth.

Millwall were the visitors to Bramall Lane on 28 March. Millwall led 0-2 by half-time. Paul Garner and Bob Hatton scored second-half goals, but the Blades lost 2-3. It was United's third home defeat of the season. The fans were unhappy, as were the players, although both groups still thought the season could be salvaged.

The Tuesday night game three days later was another home match, against Barnsley, drawing the biggest league gate of the season – 20,369. John Matthews scored in the 1-1 draw. The away tie at Colchester finished in the same scoreline, Wiggan scoring for United this time.

The Blades were now 14th in the table but the three teams below them – Fulham, Colchester United and Carlisle United – were equal with United on points. Only goal difference separated them. Newport County, Gillingham and Oxford United were all just two points behind.

Paul Garner and Don Givens scored the goals that gave United a 2-0 win against Chester, but it was becoming clear that there was growing cause for concern. Peters refused to accept the possibility that his team could get dragged into a relegation dogfight, believing he and his players were too good for that – maybe too big for the unthinkable to happen.

A 1-0 defeat at Plymouth Argyle was followed by a 1-1 draw with Brentford. Peters' signing Don Givens scored the goal, his third since joining the Blades. The point left United 15th with three games to play. Fulham, Hull City and Walsall were the remaining fixtures.

Fulham were in 11th place and had won two of their last three games. Walsall hadn't won in four games and Hull City had won once in their last 14 and had been struggling all season, so Blades fans expected to beat at least two of them, particularly as two of the last three games were at Bramall Lane.

Rumours were circulating, not for the first time, that Tony Kenworthy was of interest to Norwich City, and there was still talk of Martin Peters walking away from the job that he had inherited much earlier than he expected.

Kenworthy confirms the speculation was true: 'I was just going into Victoria Wine Bar on Ecclesall Road, for some dinner. Peters drove past in his Ford Granada, and shouted "I need you to come to my house at six o'clock tonight." When I got there, he was sat in the living room in his carpet slippers. He didn't even get up out of his chair, didn't offer me a cup of tea even, just said, "I've sold you to Norwich at the end of the season," and that was it.'

On paper, the Fulham match was certainly the most difficult of the final three games, and they came to Bramall Lane on a Tuesday night, 21 April. When Fulham went ahead there was a palpable nervousness among the 10,000 fans inside the ground, and among the players. Bob Hatton scored for United, but the night ended in a 1-2 defeat.

Top-of-the-league Rotherham United had only managed a draw with bottom club Hull City the previous night, and

Walsall gained a point at Huddersfield Town, adding more pressure. United were still four places above the drop zone, but the points gap between them and Colchester United, who were fourth from bottom, was now just three. The bottom four would go down.

Struggling Hull City were United's next opponents, and a win would give the Blades breathing space. United's travelling supporters were in good voice before the game, in particular aiming their wit at Hull striker Edwards. 'You're going down, we're not,' was among the more printable chants.

Mike Trusson scored for the Blades, but Hull earned their second draw in consecutive games when the contest ended 1-1. No prizes for guessing who scored Hull's goal.

Results elsewhere that day seemed to conspire against the Blades as well, as Walsall beat Swindon Town 2-1.

On 2 May 1981, United went into the final game of the season knowing that just a point at home to Walsall would be enough to secure their safety. Even in the unlikely event that the game finished in a defeat, if other results went their way, they could survive. Walsall needed nothing less than a win to stay up.

The plan was clear – whatever you do, just don't lose!

On the day of the game, Blades fans were surprised to see Tony Kenworthy's name missing from the team sheet. Boss Peters claimed that his player was injured. Just the luck United did not need.

Kenworthy was not injured. He was in the changing room, putting on his kit, ready to play. Peters, who had been outside the changing room door, chatting to a couple of directors, came in and told him he needed a word, gesturing towards the toilets. It was then that Peters told Kenworthy, 'You're not playing. I've told you, I've sold you to Norwich. You're not in my team.'

Paul Casey, who had broken into the team and played three games prior to the draw with Brentford, came back into the side in front of Steve Conroy in goal. Conroy, Casey, Paul Garner, Les Tibbott, Stewart Houston, John MacPhail, John Matthews, Mike Trusson, Don Givens, Bob Hatton and John Ryan were the 11 players selected by Peters to start the game.

The game itself was poor, and neither side looked like scoring. Out of the blue, MacPhail fouled Walsall striker Alan Buckley and gave away a clumsy penalty in the last five minutes. Don Penn stepped up and put the ball straight down the middle, scoring for Walsall.

Suddenly, Sheffield United found themselves in the bottom four and, for the first time, were staring in the face the very real possibility that they might be relegated.

Paul Garner had experienced the misfortune of being a Huddersfield player at the start of his career as the Terriers fell from the First Division to the Fourth. He left Huddersfield for United when the Blades were a First Division team; now he faced the reality of history repeating itself.

Remarkably, when it looked to be all over, Bob Hatton's cross was judged to have struck a hand. United were awarded a penalty. A lifeline.

Score the penalty and stay up – sending Walsall down. Miss and Walsall survive – United fall through the trap door.

It seemed an age between the referee pointing to the spot and the ball being placed on it. There was some confusion about who should take it. There is a common misperception that John Matthews had been given the role of penalty-taker. He hadn't. With Peters springing the surprise about his team selection on the players at such short notice, it was overlooked. Bad planning on the manager's part. The team had made plans during the week and practised with Kenworthy taking the penalties. He had already scored six times from the spot during the season. Now, with the future of the club hanging in the balance, Kenworthy was sitting in the dugout. All he could do now was watch and hope.

The assumption was that John Matthews would take it, but it was not his job. He was a player with a lot of experience, and could thump a ball, but on the day, he just didn't fancy it. He hadn't taken a penalty for more than a year.

It takes courage to hold your hands up in a situation like that and say 'I am not confident enough to take it'. It takes even greater courage to be the one that does step up, under that sort of pressure, with the consequences hanging on it. To know that the worst day in the club's entire history could depend on that one kick.

The man who did so was Don Givens. Had Kenworthy been playing, he would have undoubtedly had the bravery to take it, and most United fans would tell you that they'd have put their house on him putting it away. Kenworthy is confident he would have scored too. He was not an option.

With virtually the last kick of the season, Givens stepped up and struck the ball poorly. It lacked power and direction and the Walsall keeper Ron Green saved it easily.

Seconds later, the referee blew his whistle amid furious scenes in the crowd. Fans ran on to the pitch, confronting players of both teams. There were reports that fans even ran down the players' tunnel and into the dressing room. They could not believe United had been relegated: refused to accept it.

Suddenly, rumours circulated that Swindon Town had lost, and the Blades had escaped the humiliation. More fans ran on to the pitch to celebrate. Unfortunately, as we all now know, Swindon Town had drawn 0-0 at home to Brentford, a result that kept them in the division and Sheffield United were relegated to the basement of the Football League for the first time ever.

As reality set in, grown men sat in their seats, or on the floor, crying. The shame and devastation for the fans was absolutely unbearable. Only six years earlier, Sheffield United had been one of the best teams in the country, missing out on a place in Europe by a whisker.

They had some of the most respected and most exciting players in the country. They had invested in the ground, spending money to erect the beautiful South Stand in an attempt to build an arena fit for the likes of Tony Currie and Alan Woodward to work their craft.

The decision to build that stage and the failure to stay in the top division the following year had ultimately meant having to sell the star acts that the stage was built for, and after just a couple of seasons in the second tier, they had fallen even further.

After years of being the biggest team in the city, the Blades had been humiliated at Hillsborough and seen their biggest rivals promoted. Now, 12 months on, the Owls had finished ninth in Division Two. They were now two divisions higher than the Blades.

Fans were frustrated, exasperated, upset, angry, wounded and baffled.

How could this have happened?

How could we have fallen so far, so fast?

What if we had kept Currie, or Edwards and Woodward?

What if we hadn't signed Sabella?

What if Sabella had turned out to be the player he promised to be?

What if Matthews had had the nerve to take that penalty?

What if Kenworthy hadn't been injured?

What if Kenworthy had taken that penalty, instead of Givens?

Tony Kenworthy was fit to play in that game. His version of events is very different to the claim of his manager on the day. Kenworthy insists that Peters' arrogance drove his team selection that day, and his decision to leave the penalty-taker out was a display of power, showing that he was the boss.

'He had asked me to not speak my mind in the dressing room, but I was captain. If I disagreed with what he or anyone else said, I'd say so. His decision to not play me was purely driven by him wanting to send a message; he was in charge.'

Not only did Kenworthy have the nerve and the quality to take the penalty, but he also knew how much it meant. That is not to say Don Givens didn't understand or care. He showed great courage to step up and take the kick. He just wasn't Tony Kenworthy.

Kenworthy wasn't Sheffield born, but he was certainly adopted by the city and by the fans. He understood the pain and sadness, the anger and humiliation. He was a fan. He'd been at the club in one team or another since he was 12. He loved the club, loved the players.

As it turned out, the move to Norwich City never materialised and Tony Kenworthy remained a Blade. Over the years he was linked with many big clubs; Everton, Spurs, QPR under Terry Venables. Even after the Peters era ended,

Kenworthy was still often the subject of transfer speculation. He remembers, 'I got a call from Harry Haslam, after him and Peters had both left, asking me to come to his house at Barlborough. When I arrived, he picked up the phone and said, "You need to speak to this man." It was David Pleat at Luton Town, telling me he was going to sign me. I didn't want to leave. I loved United.'

He also came close to joining Derby County, although it is not clear how close the deal was. He received a call from then Derby chairman Mike Watterson. Watterson was well known as the man who brought snooker to Sheffield. Kenworthy picked up his phone to be told, 'You'll be a Derby player in three hours,' before the phone went dead. Later that day he received an equally short call, telling him to forget the call ever happened.

He would play a big part in the next chapter of Sheffield United's story, remaining a Blade until 1986. He eventually left for Mansfield, where their head coach was his former United team-mate, Bill Dearden. He played over 100 games for Mansfield, including a memorable appearance in the Football League Trophy Final (now the Papa John's Trophy) at Wembley in 1987. Mansfield met Bristol City, and when the game finished 1-1 after extra time, 58,500 fans watched a penalty shoot-out. There were four ex-Sheffield United players involved. Paul Garner lined up alongside Kenworthy and John MacPhail took one of the Bristol penalties, and scored, but Keith Curle missed his and the tie ended up in sudden death. Tony Kenworthy took the deciding penalty, against Keith Waugh. Always brave, he, of course, scored.

He finished playing professionally in 1990 and in 1998 he briefly replaced Danny Bergara as manager of Grantham Town.

Martin Peters blamed the team following the Walsall defeat, defiantly telling them that most of them would be gone from the club soon, while he would still be there in charge. Despite his arrogance, however, he was sacked shortly afterwards. He never managed again.

Kenworthy mused, 'After we'd been relegated the team went off on a jolly to Magaluf. I didn't think we should go, but then we got a phone call saying Peters had left and Ian Porterfield was coming.'

Sometimes good things fall apart so better things can fall together – Marilyn Monroe.

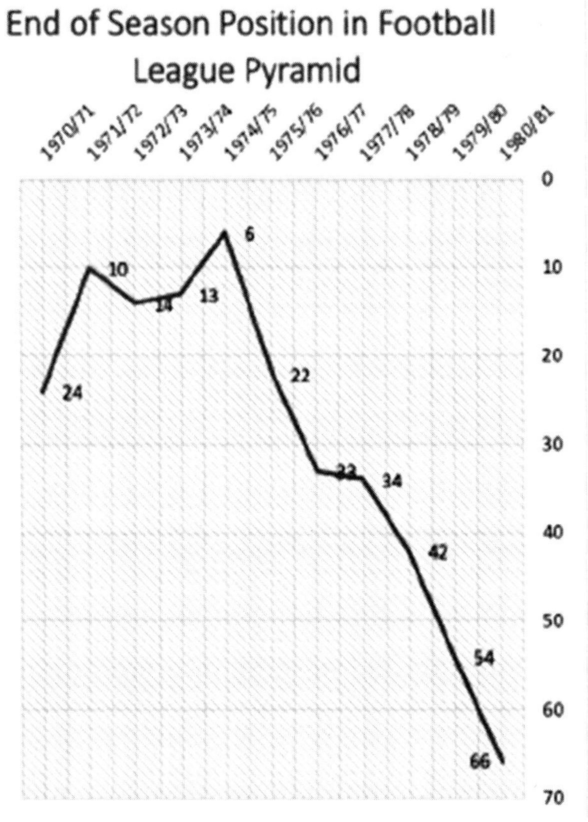

Cast

Player	Apps
Joe Shaw	714
Alan Hodgkinson	675
Alan Woodward	639
Len Badger	539
Graham Shaw	498
Cec Coldwell	478
Eddie Colquhoun	428
Tony Currie	375
John Cutbush	375
Tony Kenworthy	350
Brian Richardson	336
Gerry Summers	305
Derek Pace	302
Paul Garner	297
Keith Edwards *	293
Ted Hemsley	292
Gil Reece	225
John Flynn	224
Mick Speight	223
Geoff Salmons	207
Bill Dearden	204
Jim Brown	203
Keith Kettleborough	183
Mick Jones	172

Colin Franks	170
John MacPhail	169
Ken Mallender	169
Tony Wagstaff	164
Bernard Shaw	161
Mike Trusson	155
Steve Charles	144
Frank Barlow	137
Steve Conroy	135
Keith Eddy	134
Barry Wagstaff	126
David Munks	124
Alan Birchenall	123
John Matthews	121
Barry Hartle	117
Bob Hatton	114
Gary Hamson	108
Les Tibbott	100
Alex Sabella	88
John Tudor	78
Chris Guthrie	77
Tony Field	75
Derek Richardson	55
Gary Brazil	50
Don Givens	12
Pedro Verdi	11
Ian Benjamin	8
Alan Warboys	7

*Keith Edwards in two spells

EPILOGUE

Ain't Got a Barrel of Money. Sheffield United

I HAVE absolutely loved writing this book. You often hear people talking about Sheffield United as a family, but I never realised just how true that was – until I started talking to the players and to you, the fans.

It has amazed me how many of the supporters have real-life memories of times when they were lucky enough to meet their heroes. As Alan Biggs alluded to in this book's foreword, I was incredibly awestruck at the thought of speaking to the players. I am still awestruck!

Every single one of the players I approached happily gave their time generously. There were some marvellously moving moments, and some that were simply unprintable. There were some funny moments too. I often found myself ringing one player, and by the end of the call, I'd not only got some great anecdotes, but an additional phone number. On one such occasion an ex-player gave me the number of another and he called me the next day to tell me he'd cleared it and I was OK to call. When I called the other player, though, he was confused. 'Jason, I'm not sure what's going on here, I thought Jamie Hoyland was phoning me!'

All the players talked warmly about their former team-mates, and all have a real lasting affection for the football club. Sheffield United really is a proper club.

There was also sadness writing this book. I first started writing *Ain't Got a Barrel of Money* over two years ago, and the first Blade I spoke to was the wonderful Ted Hemsley. He kindly agreed to not only talk to me, but suggested we set up an afternoon meeting, and he would also invite his lifelong friend Len Badger. Devastatingly, Covid-19 put paid to that, and with social distancing preventing the meeting taking place, it never happened. Before restrictions were lifted, Len tragically passed away.

I never got to meet Len Badger, and this should serve as a reminder to all of us that these people – these stars that we adore (and occasionally criticise or boo, depending on the result!) – are human beings, mortals, and will one day no longer walk among us. Let's make sure that their stories will never be lost.

Make the most of every day and count your blessings for the memories that the players at the club you love have brought you in the past and will do again in the future …

UTB

Thanks again for reading.

Jason